Bound to Differ

The Dynamics of Theological Discourses

Also by Wesley A. Kort

Shriven Selves: Religious Problems in Recent American Fiction (1972)
Narrative Elements and Religious Meaning (1975)
Moral Fiber: Character and Belief in Recent American Fiction (1982)
Modern Fiction and Human Time: A Study in Narrative and Belief (1985)
Story, Text, and Scripture: Literary Interests in Biblical Narrative (1988)

BOUND to DIFFER

The Dynamics of Theological Discourses

Wesley A. Kort

The Pennsylvania State University Press
University Park, Pennsylvania

Library of Congress Cataloging-in-Publication Data

Kort, Wesley A.
Bound to differ : the dynamics of theological discourses / Wesley A. Kort.

p. cm.
Includes bibliographical references and index.
ISBN 0-271-00859-8
1. Language and languages—Religious aspects—Christianity.
2. Theology—Methodology. 3. Discourse analysis. I. Title.
BR115.L25K66 1992
230'.014—dc20 91-44464
CIP

Printed in the United States of America

It is the policy of The Pennsylvania State University Press to use acid-free paper for the first printing of all clothbound books. Publications on uncoated stock satisfy the minimum requirements of American National Standard for Information Sciences—Permanence of Paper for Printed Library Materials, ANSI Z39.48–1984.

CONTENTS

PREFACE

MOST OF MY WORK IN RELIGION and literary studies has been aimed at questioning the autonomy of modernist texts and the prevailing critical methods that conspire to reinforce the notion of autonomy. This interrogation takes the form not so much of relating literary studies to other interests—social, cultural, and religious— but of arguing that such interests always are there already, inseparable from interests claimed to be "literary."

However, in both my immediately preceding book and in this one, I turn my attention more directly to religious studies. My previous book treated biblical studies, and it both gave support to recent literary interests in biblical narrative and attacked such interests by claiming that they are not literary enough, that they are, in fact, motivated by an attempt to subject biblical texts to already institutionalized literary-critical methods. I tried to demonstrate that biblical narratives, by virtue of their complexity and variability, could not so easily be domesticated. The augmentation of biblical criticism with literary interests, which is very much happening these days, has not, unfortunately, had the effect of complicating the work of religious studies but of placing next to them competing literary practices and theories. The direction of the book was against this distinction and the "coherence by partition" it fostered.

I continue this project by turning now to Christian theology. Again I use literary interests to describe this work as more complex and variable and less coherent than it at first may seem or may be taken by its practitioners and readers to be.[1] The ending of both the preceding book and of this one lead, by separate routes, to what in my conclusion I call a culture of scripture and belief.

The topic of this study is theological conflict. While that is a topic more fully brought into view by literary than by theological interests, it is also a topic that arises from my exposure from youth on to theology. I grew up in an environment where theology divided people, at times even ending speaking relationships within families. Theological hostility and conflict were touted as inevitable, even virtuous. "Rotten wood won't split" was the excuse. People who did not hold and articulate sharp and nonnegotiable theological distinctiveness were judged as lacking conviction. Tentativeness and tolerance were identified with indifference. When I moved from that Dutch Calvinist theological environment to the Divinity School of the University of Chicago, the theological "orthodoxy" there was process theology, especially in the plain and pared form given it by Professor Bernard Loomer, whom most of the theological students followed. Theological alternatives to this position were alienated or dismissed, and I responded by internalizing the conflict. Devotees of process theology, while they failed at the time to convince me, forced me to take their position seriously and to recognize its difference from the theology of my background. My involvement in theology was, subsequently, highly personal, and it took the form of asking what kind of relation to one another such differing Christian formulations as traditional Calvinism and Hartshornean process theology might have. Differences of this kind, I soon realized, were irreconcilable, and I negotiated a relation between them, first, in a book (*Shriven Selves: Religious Problems in Recent American Fiction,* 1972) about fictions with narrators having analogous problems and solving them not theologically but by the inclusiveness of their narrative discourses and, second, by positing separable kinds of Christian theological traditions, along the lines suggested by Reinhold Niebuhr in his discussion of the separation occurring in the Reformation/Renaissance between the language of divine grace and the language of human initiative.[2]

The matter has been brought to my attention again by recent changes in the theological climate in this country that have even affected my own university. Increasingly aggressive and confident voices utter disdain for a "liberal" theological milieu. Here is a theology that not only in style but also in substance makes much of difference and opposition.

I am, therefore, aware not so much of Christian theology in the singular as of theologies in the plural, not so much of theological conversation as of theological conflict and exclusion. I take theological differences as basic, consequently, and in this book I clarify why. I propose that differences are not accidental but central to Christian theology itself and that without these differences there would be little if any theology as we know it. We tend to think of difference as superficial and accidental rather than as causal and constitutive, but I shall argue that to understand Christian theology an appreciation for the strategies and dynamics of difference and opposition is indispensable.

My interest in this matter would not have developed in the form it has taken here, had it not been for my introduction to discourse analysis. Discourse analysis provided me most of all with a way to recognize that theological discourses depend on difference. It gave me a sense of the oppositional character of discourse and of the characteristics of power always attached to meaning. This meant that my conclusions about the causal status of conflict in theological discourse and of the power these discourses generate in order to exclude and discredit what within other theological positions threatens them could be articulated and would have support. Discourse analysis provided me with a way to sustain an analysis that I had begun long ago.

There are several people who have read parts or the whole of this work, and I want to thank them for their interest and encouragement without making them liable for whatever weaknesses readers may find here: Ken Surin and Bob Osborn, colleagues here at Duke; three graduate students, Ray Person, Kristina Swenson, and Sean Butler, who all have strong interests in discourse analysis and social theory; and friends at other institutions, Terrence W. Tilley of the Religion Department at Florida State University, Philip Rolnick of the Religion and Philosophy Department at Greensboro College, and David Jasper, now of the English Department at the University of Glasgow.

Finally, I want to thank the provost of Duke University, Professor Thomas A. Langford, for the grant made available by him to me for the partial subvention of this publication. Even more than the grant, I treasure the confidence in and encouragement of my work that he has expressed in many ways since the day, so long ago now, when, as chairman of my department, he hired me.

Wesley A. Kort
Fall 1991

INTRODUCTION

THE WAY OF READING CHRISTIAN theologies that I propose in this study is warranted, if not required, by discourse analysis specifically and, more generally, by the current critical ambiance that so-called postmodernist assumptions and interests provide. This context supports the practice of treating a theological discourse not so much in relation to its speaker or referents, or in and by itself, or as an instance of "creative *bricolage*,"[1] but, rather, in relation to other theological discourses. These relations are primarily negative, relations of competition, opposition, and even repression. My purpose in this study is to view Christian theology in terms of such dynamics. The underlying proposal is that Christian theologies cannot be adequately or accurately read if these dynamics are ignored. This proposal works against the grain of theological discourses themselves because those discourses conceal, by the attention they draw to other things, the determining and basic role these dynamics play in generating force and significance.

Christian theology, while noticeably marked by diversity and polemic, usually is taken to be a unified and affirmative enterprise. This assumption resides in the use of the singular noun and in an adjective that suggests shared beliefs. Difference and conflict are relegated to the surface of theology or to its periphery. Christian theology basically or centrally, it is assumed, constitutes a single discourse inclusive of its diversity, and differences among Christian theologians are taken to be either unnecessary or unproductive.

My purpose in this study is to show that difference and conflict, rather than accidental or peripheral, are unavoidable and central to the theological enterprise and that theology, rather than unified, is basically divided and conflicted. Differences and conflicts, rather than belonging to the effects of theology, are among its very causes; they serve to determine theological argumentation. When attention is shifted *from* that to which theologies refer and the sources or voices that claim to warrant them and *to* the ways in which and the reasons why theologies differ from and conflict with one another, one can see that these differences and the conflicts that result from them are discursively productive. Theological discourses depend upon a play of differences and conflicts that must be taken into account if they are to be accurately read.

While it is true that every discourse differs from every other one, many differences are relatively inconsequential. The theological differences that seem really to matter, that give rise or can be attributed to those dynamics that largely account for theological force and significance, are of a limited and specific kind, and it is my purpose to identify not all but only such basic differences, to account for why they are unavoidable, and to reveal how they come into play.

In order to display this matter, two quite separable tasks must be undertaken. The first is to clarify and deploy a mode of analysis made possible by freeing theological discourses from ties that deflect attention from the dynamics of differences and the role of conflicts among theologies. When we attend to a discourse we usually turn toward that to which the discourse refers, or we evaluate the voice or source that warrants the discourse, or both. Indeed, theological discourses direct attention to important, even ultimate, issues, and it is to be expected that the reader will be less interested in the discourse itself than in the reality, plausibility, or other qualities of that about which theology speaks. It is also not surprising that readers should attend to the voice or the source of theology, since theologies often depend upon or reveal extraordinary sources—the faith or beliefs of the speaker, some revelation or insight granted either to the sponsor as individual or as community, or the institution the theologian represents. A way of reading that severs the ties of discourses to referents and sources and turns attention to the relation of discourses to one another needs to be justified, and I attempt to do that in the first half of this study.

The second task is to give readings of theologies that will disclose in them the dynamics of differences and conflicts, dynamics that allow us both to distinguish theologies from one another and to trace how differences among them generate significance and force. The mode of analysis that I deploy in the first part I employ in the second to demonstrate its utility as a way of reading theologies. This demonstration occupies the second half of this study. Theologies will be read as products of the differences and the conflicts potentially or actually arising among them. It will show how theologies can be read not as "about" that to which they refer nor even "about" their sources, sponsors, or voices but as "about" one another. The examples are far from exhaustive, and they are not used to illustrate all theological work possible or actual. I have not attempted to cover the theological waterfront but, rather, to illustrate my principal points and to demonstrate this way of reading. I do hope, however, that these examples are not whimsical and that they will have a centrifugal effect, for I believe that this kind of analysis and interpretation is not limited to these examples but can be applied with similar results to other moments of the recent theological situation, to Christian theological traditions, and, perhaps, even to the dynamics of theological discourses in other religious traditions.

The first part of the study is theoretical. It provides reasons why theological discourses can be severed from their relations to referents and sources and related to one another. It then adapts "discourse analysis" to the task of isolating components of theological discourses that account for differences and generate conflicts. This part, no less than the second, is selective and limited, for "discourse analysis" is in itself far from a single or simple strategy or mode of study. The complexity arises from its multidisciplinary sources; although originating in the social sciences, it represents a range of other interests, including philosophy of language and literary theory. In addition, discourse analysis must be distinguished from similar or related, but separable, interests such as "conversation analysis" and "intertextuality." Within discourse analysis itself, furthermore, lies a range of differing political interests and objectives. Some discourse analysis maintains a political neutrality by describing quite formal qualities of discursive situations, but discourse analysis can also be political; it can emphasize the issues of power and privilege that are built into discursive situations and how discourses are granted authority because of their institutional bases and the social and political powers they serve or that produce them. Discourse analysis can become itself political by exposing concealed political and social interests in discourses and challenging imbalances of privilege that may structure discursive situations.

In this study I take a middle pose on the relation of discourse analysis to political interests and questions. I treat discourses and discursive situations as always conditioned by power and marked by political implications and potentials, but I do not treat theological discourses as concealments or defenses of social, economic, and political advantages. Discursive situations, including those that are recognizably theological, include force as well as significance, and power produces and legitimates inequalities, repressions and exclusions. Any theological situation, therefore, favors some participants over others; discourse is always going on in some way already, and some discourses are likely to be dominating the field at the expense of others. This means that a theological discourse does not become part of a "game" in which the necessity and legitimacy of theological opponents is assumed and protected. Indeed, a theological discourse will attempt to discredit those potential or actual theological discourses it opposes so as to expel them from consideration and, more importantly, to conceal the fact that it depends for its force and significance on its contrary relation to those rejected and resisted discourses. The situation, it appears, is less like a game than like a war. Theologies and the institutional, political, and social investments they, like any other discourses, carry, validate, and reinforce must be seen in their actually or potentially violent relations to one another if they are to be adequately analyzed and interpreted.

However, while I am attentive to the force of theological discourses, to the ways in which they oppose, exclude, and repress actual or potential alternatives to them, and to the reasons why theologies carry persistent political implications, I do not exchange theological discourses for their institutional, political, social, or economic bases and consequences. I do not argue that what I have called "concealment" in theological discourses, the way in which their dependence on those discourses with which they differ is ignored or denied, is always actually a concealment of another kind, namely, the cloaking of political and economic advantages and ambitions in the language of theological polemics. While I recognize that this may often occur, I interpret the matters of power and concealment, dominance and repression, as ways also of gaining *theological* advantage, even though they may, perhaps usually will, grant advantages of other kinds. The middle pose struck here, then, takes theological discourses neither as abstracted from and transcendent to the dynamics of difference and conflict, nor as cloaks that cover the advancement and protection of social, political, and economic advantages. The two alternatives that, like Scylla and Charybdis, I try to move between can be referred to pejoratively as "reification" and "reduction." If forced to choose, I would declare my sympathies with a stress on the social and political conditions of discourses, for these have too long been ignored. But I want to place my discussion between the alternatives to show that theological ideas and the forms of theological discourses (to use terms congenial to the formal side) can and should be read as the results or anticipations of opposition, conflict, and force (to use terms congenial to the political side). This will clarify, it is hoped, how meaning and power in theological discourses are inseparable from one another, even though many readers discount or ignore either the one or the other ingredient in this compound. By making this neither a formal nor a political study of theology, I may easily end with no sympathetic readers at all. But that is usually the risk in resisting polarization and the recognizable identity that one of these clear alternatives would provide.

The theologies described in the second part will, I hope, reveal the conflicts that I think are so interesting and productive. Whole categories of theologies have not been included, and the reasons for some of these omissions will be given later in the study. Selection of texts as examples is never a neutral process, and I realize that selection limits the scope and veracity of the argument as much as supports it. But that is also always a price to be paid. Complicating the selection process are a number of variables. First, theologians and theological texts are considered because of the "basic beliefs" they appear to deploy, beliefs that are not derived and constructed but assumed and defended, beliefs that are "basic" both in the sense that they give rise to other beliefs and in the sense that they are not always conscious or explicit.[2] Michel Foucault uses "governing statements" to refer to root components of a discourse that constitute a strategic choice but leave room for the greatest number of subsequent options, statements "that put into operation rules of formation in their most extended form."[3] Not only do theologians differ as to their basic beliefs or governing statements; readers may also not agree as to what in the work of a particular theologian I take the basic beliefs and governing statements to be. In addition, some of the theologians or texts treated are more difficult to analyze as to basic beliefs and governing statements than are others. Finally, the entire corpus of a theologian may be determined by the same basic beliefs and governing statements, and the differences and conflicts needed for their articulation, but other theologians seem to be more topically governed and to shift starting points as they move from one project to another. At times, then, it is easier to speak of the continued output of a theologian and, at other times, to concentrate on a single text. I have not often recounted shifts in the careers of theologians or reasons why they have "changed their minds." So, the part on examples is troubled both by the difficulty of selecting, of including some and not others, and by the various ways the work of particular theologians has been treated.

An important *theological* question comes from the relations of the two parts of the book to one another. The question concerns the relation of the *specific* language of Christian theologies, characteristic of the second part, to the *general* language of discourse analysis in the first. Some theological readers may object, saying that the specific language of Christian faith, even in theological formulations, cannot be analyzed and interpreted in general categories. Again, I hope to strike a middle pose. I do not dissolve the particular languages of Christian theologies into general categories of discourse analysis as though those categories preexist the theologies and are manifested in them, but I also do not argue that particular Christian theologies are free and immune from such description and analysis, since they also constitute a discursive situation. This applies not only to my analysis of theologies but also to the terms employed by theologies. For example, I do not say that "God," as a word used by a Christian, is a particular term in a general category of language about the "transcendent" or the "sacred," but I also would not say that "God," as a word used by a Christian, must be taken only as applicable to specific instances of Christian worship or witness to revelation. I propose, instead, that the significance of that word arises from the play of inclusion and separation between the specific instances and the category. Theologians depend upon, while they may also repudiate, the general category of language about the transcendent, let us say, for the force and significance of their particular uses of the word "God," and theologians will differ from one another as to whether and to what degree they include the particular within the general or distinguish the particular word and use from the general category. I want not to dissolve these differences but, rather, to embed them in the work. To do that I must avoid an a priori decision on the question of the dependence/separation of Christian theologies from theories of discourse more generally conceived. Nor do I want to solve the problem by an inner/outer distinction or a distinction between first and second orders of discourse. While such distinctions at times are helpful, they do not and cannot resolve the tension between the immunity of Christian theological discourses from and their vulnerability to general language categories and theories, the tension between the dependence of theological discourses on and their independence from the dynamics characteristic of other discourses, or the differences among theologies in their formulations of and reactions to these moments of dependence/independence.

The question also arises as to the relation of the theological discourses of Christianity to other Christian discourses, such as ecclesiastical discourses—articles in church publications, meetings of church leaders, and discussions among members in church educational situations—and liturgical discourses, such as sermons and prayers.[4] This is not a matter that I shall pursue. First, it is a rather easy distinction to make because the occasions and settings of these kinds of discourses are sufficiently separable. Furthermore, there is too much variation among the theologies that I consider—as to their institutional placement and their relevance to the ecclesial-institutional and liturgical discourses of those institutions—to establish constants in this regard. While it may be important to distinguish liturgical, ecclesial, or institutional discourses from theological discourses, this is not a matter of equal importance across the theological examples that I shall consider, and it is, in any case, a distinction that, when appropriate to make, can be made quite directly. The dynamics that govern the relations among theological, ecclesial, and liturgical languages are, while worth comparing, specific to traditions, institutions, or communities.

Readers are likely to expect that in the conclusion I shall state some kind of theological position in response to or based on the study of theological difference and conflict. They will be disappointed. In the conclusion I do not resolve the tensions or conflicts among theological discourses that are exposed by the study or choose one from among the principal kinds of theology I have analyzed. In fact, attempts to resolve theological differences will be questioned in the conclusion. Readers who know my previous work may expect that, if I do not resolve the question with a theological position, I will turn to narrative as providing coherence in the face of theological dissonance. But that is also a move I do not make, although a "narrative theology," one construed differently from those now largely available, can provide an antidote to the present situation created by propositional theologies. But I am just as eager to point out that a narrative, because it also is discourse, participates in the play of differences and in the situation of conflict. No, I end with the situation of differences and conflicts, one I characterize, however, in a positive mode. I suggest that the language or culture of differences and conflict can and should be seen also as the language or culture of scripture and belief.

PART I

THEOLOGICAL DISCOURSES

Theory and Model

1

Discourse Analysis

Meaning and Power

TO EMPLOY DISCOURSE ANALYSIS, as this study does, albeit in a general way, is to enter a discursive situation that is itself complex and even conflicted. While it is not germane to this study fully to address the present state and methodological issues concerning discourse analysis, its roots and fruits, it is necessary to clarify a few things, particularly assumptions about language basic to this kind of analysis, its relation to similar, even overlapping forms of analysis, and the emphasis that discourse analysis leads or compels one to make concerning the relation of a discourse to political and institutional questions and factors. I shall look briefly at these matters to make some methodological distinctions and to suggest what or how much shall be made of political factors in this study.

I

Direct access to discourse analysis, to its relation to other scholarly interests, and to its implications for a study of theology becomes available when we ask the question of how discourses receive or generate their meaning and authority, force, or power. The first answer to that question is widely shared among those who practice inquiries of this kind. After that, important differences occur. The first answer is primarily a negative one. I shall describe it briefly now and develop it more fully, particularly in its implications for theology, in the opening pages of the next chapter.

In a word, the shared assumption in work of this kind is that discourse should be taken as deriving or generating its meaning and authority in its relations of dependence and independence, similarity and differences, or confirmation and opposition to other discourses. This assumption implies as its negative a discounting or dismissal of traditional answers as to the sources or causes of meaning and authority in discourses.

We are accustomed to thinking that discourses receive or develop meaning and authority from that to which they refer. It is the significance and importance of its referent that confer these qualities on a discourse, and such qualities are detectable in or attributed to a discourse to the degree that it directs attention to, defers to, or faithfully represents that to which it refers. Discourse analysis not only turns attention away from this traditional way of accounting for meaning and authority and directs it toward the relation of discourses to other discourses; it also implies or proposes by such a turn that meaning and authority do not inhere in the referent but are ascribed to the referent by the discourse. "Referents" are significant, important, valuable, or authoritative because discourses make them so.

We are also accustomed to thinking that discourses derive their meaning and authority from their speakers and sources. The learning, integrity, credentials, office, qualities of character or mind, and other attributes of speakers confer on discourses, it is generally thought, the meaning and authority that they have or convey. But discourse analysis turns away from this way of accounting for the significance and power of discourse toward the relation of discourses to one another and, in so doing, implies or proposes that the authority and significance of the voice or source of a discourse is established by the discourse itself. In other words, one major function of a discourse, it is argued, is to advance norms that will grant its voice or source power and significance. Discourses contain within them, perhaps have as their principal ingredient, reasons why their sources are to be taken as having authority.

Finally, more recently and perhaps less frequently, it has become customary to attribute the authority and meaning of a discourse to patterns, systems, and structures that antedate discourses and legitimate them, rules of logic and grammar or social and linguistic codes and structures. Again, discourse analysis, by turning attention to the relations among discourses, implies that such rules, patterns, structures, and systems are projected and warranted by discourses, rather than the other way around. Like referent and voice, structure, code, system, and the like are seen more as products than as causes, more as determined than determining, more secondary than primary. In other words, at all three of these points—referent, voice, or structure—discourse analysis assumes or effects an exchange; what is ordinarily and traditionally taken as generative of significance, validity, and authority becomes secondary and derived.

It is important to note that this exchange is not dictated by discourses themselves. If discourses appear to derive their meaning and power primarily from referents, voice, and system, it is very important for their power and meaning to conceal that they derive their power and meaning not in those ways but, rather, from their relations to one another. This means that discourse analysis goes against the grain of a discourse and exposes a situation that, for the sake of a discourse's power and meaning, is concealed.

It also follows that discourse analysis is not exclusively or even primarily interested in the acknowledged or obvious dynamics of citation, polemic, and other interactive relations of discourses with one another. While not irrelevant, obvious points of dependence, difference, or conflict are less in need of analysis than are those that are concealed or unrecognized.

Of even less interest are more formal and internal ways of accounting for meaning and power in a discourse. While discourse analysis does not relate discourses first of all to something outside of them—referents, voices, or social and linguistic systems—this does not mean that attention is given to discourses in their autonomy, their own rhetorical strategies, for example. Rather, it turns attention to the relations of dependence and independence, or confirmation and opposition among discourses. It brings to attention the dynamics of those relations, particularly negative relations to one another, and the way these relations generate meaning and power.

Because attention is turned by discourse analysis primarily to differences and oppositions among discourses as a way of accounting for meaning and authority, it follows that this form of analysis places more emphasis on power than do the other, more customary ways of accounting for meaning and authority. It assumes or posits a close relation between meaning and power, and it takes the production of meaning out of the uplifted or protected realm of facts, minds, and language into a world of social interaction. It relates the study of meaning to the complex of human interactions and the social influence that some discourses are able to generate or possess.

One of the consequences of this close tie between meaning and power in discourses is that analysis of this kind develops within itself differing attitudes concerning the relations of meaning and power to one another. Specifically, discourse analysis, by countering idealist and empiricist notions of how meaning and authority are produced and conveyed, raises the question of the contrary premise, namely, whether the production of meaning and authority should be accounted for in social, political, or economic ways. Even more, it raises the question of whether the apparent meanings of discourses are really the occasions, coverings, or justifications for positions of power sought, gained, or protected. Next, then, to be addressed should be the relation of meaning to power in the dynamics of discursive situations.

II

It is not surprising that discourse analysis, in its placement of discourses in a social matrix of relations and interactions, finds its principal location in the social sciences.[1] The focus of major attention is human interaction, face to face exchanges, and discourse as conversation becomes central. Questions such as these are asked: How are the limits set as to what can or should be said in particular situations? What determines the share of the event each participant can or should take? How and when does each participant know when it is or should be his or her turn to speak? This can be called conversation analysis; it emphasizes the dynamics of verbal interactions in their interdependent relations within socially framed situations. Conversations are observable social occasions, and attempts can be made to derive patterns and even tacit rules from multiple cases.

Analysis of this kind, while largely distant from the sort undertaken in this study, provides an important point by focusing attention on discourse as interaction. The situation is multiple, the discourses are affected by one another, and it is necessary, in order to understand a single discourse, to see it in relation to the entire discursive situation of interaction. Discourses are related to one another as constituting a dynamic social situation.

The majority of conversations, however, have a positive social purpose or effect—to reinforce relationships, to convey information, to reach agreement on a plan of action, and the like. A minority of conversations are manifestly agonistic, or directed toward disagreement and conflict. While such occur, social situations or structures characterized by such interactions—families, for example—can be judged as dysfunctional. As Donald Allen and Rebecca Guy put it, "verbal exchange is satisfying and rewarding to both actors because it tends to reduce dissonance, give social support, and provide further information for future action."[2]

In addition, conversation analysis is less analytic and interpretive and more descriptive than discourse analysis. It is directed toward the complexities of interactions among two or more participants, particularly how those interactions are made possible, sustained, framed, and made productive. Diverse factors are involved in such events, and there are many kinds of occasions for conversations, so many, in fact, that the question arises for such researchers as to whether or not conversations are studiable.[3] One can understand that such research is directed more to the dynamics of interaction than to the discourses themselves.

Finally, conversation analysis, because it is directed toward deriving general patterns and theories from studies of particular conversations, tends to downplay social differences among participants that become very important in discourse analysis. This tendency is supported by the fact that live conversations, as already noted, tend to be situations in which it is most often appropriate to downplay or even bracket differences. Teachers talking with students, supervisors with workers, owners with users, parents with children, etc.: such situations, while marked by sharp inequalities of authority and privilege, are generally marked as well by a need to reduce the importance of those inequalities so that trust will be secured, information passed, plans made, etc. Discourse analysis, on the other hand, stresses differences and is attentive to the social and political conditions that structure and determine discursive situations. This, along with the stress in conversation analysis on positive social purposes and effects and on its descriptive methods, allows a distinction to be drawn between it and discourse analysis.

Another important characteristic of discourse analysis is its greater attention to texts of various kinds rather than to live verbal interactions, as in conversation analysis. There are several reasons for this emphasis. One of these is the interest in what is already there, on the textual context that already gives content, shape, or direction to a discursive situation. Written discourse enters a situation in which other discourses are obviously already there, affecting the status and significance of the entering text. The situation is always loaded or shaped in advance. In addition, the stress on textuality greatly extends or enlarges the discursive situation, and discourse analysis is marked by a tendency to bring into focus or to call attention to inclusive social situations, to totalities rather than to isolated instances of verbal interaction. Finally, it can be said that texts may have stronger political and economic implications than live interactions. There are costs in producing a text, so that textual discourse is more clearly marked politically and economically, selected and supported, for example, by some institution. Furthermore, there is often in writing and publication the need to justify the production of a text, and that takes the form of displacing former or competing texts, to herald this text's superiority and to downplay its dependence on other texts. The relations of texts to one another, then, are more dissonant than live conversations generally are.

This emphasis on texts raises the question of the relation of discourse analysis to that form of literary study called "intertextuality." Involved in study of this kind is the attempt to trace and account for the evidences of other texts in a particular text. The effect is to subvert the notion that texts are autonomous and unified. The power and significance of a text lie in its relation to other texts that are included within it, and these often-called "interests" are not recognized by the text as borrowed and are subsumed by the text so that the reader's response to such "interests" is controlled by the text.

"Intertextuality" as a form of literary analysis is more focused than is discourse analysis on the inclusion and domination of other texts by a text, on the ways in which a text is affected by the actual or threatened influence on it of other texts, and on single texts as sites of these dynamics. Discourse analysis directs attention not to single texts in their composite nature but to many texts in relations of difference and opposition. Moreover, "intertextuality" tends to be an analysis heavily influenced by psychological interests. Oedipal and other anxieties and the threat of influence often mark such work, and Michael Riffaterre, a major figure in this area, treats the relation of "intertexts" (that is, texts incorporated in and by a text) to texts as the relation of the unconscious to the conscious. Analysis of this kind, he suggests, has a psychological quality.[4]

While related in many ways to what I am describing as conversation analysis and as intertextuality, discourse analysis differs from them in the attention it gives to difference and conflict among discourses. Diane Macdonell, for example, argues that opposition is not to be numbered among the consequences of discourses but among its causes.[5] Discourses are not abstract and isolated, not free to set their own terms as though on some unoccupied, neutral terrain. There are always discourses already there that must be contended with and, perhaps, displaced. Any discourse derives its standing by means of its differences from other discourses. It is also not as though discourses arise freely from consciousness as expressions of original, prediscursive ideas. As much as they are not developed in isolation, they do not arise in abstraction. They are always agonistic; "they develop out of clashes with one another, and because of this there is a political dimension to each use of words and phrases in writing or in speech" (43). Meanings do not exist by themselves but by means of difference. They arise in positions of struggle, and words "change their meaning according to the positions from which they are used" (47). The social theory implicit in such assumptions about discourse comes to the fore in the work of Jean-François Lyotard, who calls the motto "To speak is to fight" "the first principle underlying our method as a whole."[6] The principle derives, actually, from his more basic theory concerning "the agonistic aspect of society" (16).

Discourse analysis is marked, therefore, by political interests, and it accounts for the power and significance of discourses very largely in terms, first, of the unequal footing determined by the social, economic, or political positions participants occupy and, second, by the discursive situations themselves, the sites or occasions of interactions, which often favor one or some parties in the situation at the expense of others. If conversation analysis is primarily a sociological interest and "intertextuality" primarily a psychological one, discourse analysis is principally political in directions and motivations. The primacy of political questions and factors in discourse analysis often derives support from the work of Michel

Foucault, who redefines the notion of the political and the relation of discourse to it by stressing that knowledge, because it is produced and disseminated by a matrix of institutions and practices, is inescapably and inherently political.

Politics for Foucault and for those who are influenced by him is not a particular interest but rather one that permeates the entire social and cultural analysis, not limited, for example, to specific institutions or occasions. The category of the political is broken open, and the political spills out to saturate all of the issues connected with discourse, knowledge, and their analysis. Discourse analysis itself, then, readily becomes involved in political issues, for the goal of the analysis can be to reveal relations of power, relations that those with vested interests in and built-in advantages from certain social and economic situations will want to keep concealed.

For Foucault, modernity is marked by a shift in the ways discourses, that is, power and knowledge, are institutionalized. This shift allows power to circulate through a society more thoroughly and subtly, less visibly and centrally. Power infiltrates and affects all aspects of knowledge.[7] Foucault offers a thoroughgoing analysis of the infiltration of political power into all areas of social life. Even in our bodies we feel its conditioning effects.[8] Rather than linked to some specific intention or institution or directed toward the control of some actions, power/knowledge in the modern regime is institutionalized by impersonal, pervasive, and conditioning practices and is directed toward the control of minds and reflexes.

Closely related to such political interests in discourse analysis is the complex matter of the relation of discourses to institutions. Obviously, institutions provide the settings for discourses, perhaps giving "home court" advantages to some participants and "away game" disadvantages to others. Institutions locate discourses, and they set limits to what can be undertaken and to the terms that can be used. As Jean-François Lyotard says, "[Institutions] privilege certain classes of statements (sometimes only one) whose predominance characterizes the discourse of the particular institution: there are things that should be said, and there are ways of saying them."[9]

Institutions not only house discourses; they are also, I would add, embodiments of discourses and can become the contraries for discourses that oppose them. Institutions are not simply sites for discourses. They are established with discourses cemented or sedimented in them. Discourse analysis always leads to or implies institutional analysis.

One does not, perhaps, always think of institutions as embodied or established discourses. One reason for this is that the power and significance of an institution often depends upon the concealment of the discourse that it embodies. I take this comment to be roughly equivalent to what Fredric Jameson refers to as the political unconscious.[10] It often occurs, moreover, that the recognizable or even official discourse of an institution conceals an implicit discourse that those identified with the institution do not want known or do not even recognize themselves. So, to take a quite simple example merely to make the point clear, a country club may articulate its power and significance in terms of its ability to offer recreational and social opportunities that serve its clientele, by providing the physical and personal benefits of exercise and relaxation. But there may be another discourse, a more accurate and important one, that remains hidden, namely, that the club provides people who are identifiable in specific economic, social, and political ways opportunities to meet together and, however informally, to consolidate and advance their common social, political, and economic interests. This kind of discursive complexity or duplicity seems to mark all institutions, from the clubs that children form to nations, and that range includes churches.

This concealment and duplicity creates a resource as well as a problem. As a resource it allows for the internal criticism and reformation of institutions. The hidden discourse can, for example, be challenged by the official or manifest discourse of an institution. The critic, whether from within or from without, can point out the contrary relation between what the institution declares itself to be and what it actually is. Since the declared discourse is usually a less self-serving, more ideal one, it can be used to criticize the more self-serving, perhaps even exclusive, repressive, and exploitive, side of an institution's life. As Nancy Fraser puts it, there may be a form of "critique that consists in condemning the institutions of a culture for their failure to realize [their] own widely accepted ideals."[11] The declared discourse can often be used as a norm by which to criticize the discourses concealed in the institution's actual practices.

The more powerful and significant an institution becomes, the more difficult it may be to articulate the discourses it embodies. An institution can smother its discourses and be taken for granted, and attempting to surface its discourse may seem arbitrary and artificial. An external or internal critic of an institution, then, who tries to surface a submerged discourse will appear to be more provocative than the duplicity in the institution's discursive situation. This difficulty often faces those, for example, who want to point out the latent racism or sexism of an institution. The charge, for example, that there exists a submerged racist discourse in the American legal system will strike many people as excessive and forced. The acknowledged discourse, the symbol of a blind, evenhanded justice, contradicts the attempt to identify a hidden discourse of racial discrimination and control. Furthermore, an institution may become so established that there seems to be no discourse embodied in it. It becomes simply the way things are done naturally and normally. The institutions of marriage and family, for example, have embodied in them discourses concerning gender roles and relations that feminist theorists try to surface despite the fact that these institutions are commonly thought of as in and by themselves devoid of significance and power, as deriving significance and power only from the particular relationships produced by individual marriages and families. For Jameson, who calls attention not finally to such institutions as these but to a total historical moment or period of cultural production, the deep ideological structure, hidden by the surface discourses or texts that mask it, can be analyzed only indirectly. Critique of the submerged or concealed discourses of particular institutions can probably not predict in advance the numerous ways by which duplicity is created or the ways by which these situations are to be exposed.

Institutions have the power to determine what those identified with them will believe, think, and say, what questions will and will not be raised, what will be thought of as important, what good and what bad, what true and what false.[12] Institutions can hold this kind of position because they constitute enabling fields that allow people to have identities, interests, goals, and satisfactions. The power and stability of such institutions can, at least in part, be measured by the degree to which people assume that their personal identities, interests, goals, and satisfactions are self-generated and self-possessed rather than given to them and sustained for them by institutionalized discourses that could, and, because they are partial, should, be questioned.

Institutions do not develop stability and influence simply by the voluntary association of people, therefore, as though their power and significance arose by popular assent. Although there are voluntary associations and although institutions do actively work to extend their influence by adding adherents, there seems more to be an unavoidable relation between human identity, the need, that is, for power and significance, and the ability of institutions—nation, class, church, profession, home—to provide it. Institutions thereby make subjects of their participants in all senses of that word. The participants conspire in that process because in order to have a discourse that will grant them a sense of identity, coherence, and significance they need to belong, to adopt the institutional discourse. This accounts, at least in part, for the fact that people with little economic and social power may be the most loyal participants in an institution, for example, the most patriotic, the most dedicated to factory or boss, the most reliable soldiers, the most faithful in church attendance, the most fanatical sports fans, or the most devoted to their families.

It is difficult to separate oppositional from institutional ways by which discourses generate power and significance also because institutions oppose one another, and they may have their appeal largely in the oppositional relations they hold to competing or alternative institutions. This is as true of highly voluntary institutions, such as groups of friends, as it is of nations; indeed, churches, along with businesses, football teams, and institutions of higher learning in the United States, are largely defined in contrast, even in opposition to, one another.

Another reason why oppositional forms of generating discursive power and significance are difficult to separate from institutional forms is that oppositional discourses often depend upon an institution as their target. This, indeed, is what critique and critical theory often involve. The stability that an institution provides, once its implied, concealed, or submerged discourse has been surfaced, grants power to an oppositional discourse because that discourse has a vulnerable target. In addition, such an oppositional discourse, by diverting attention to the institution it attacks, need not articulate its own implicit institutional interests. To put it another way, roughly equivalent to the status and import of an institution's submerged discourses is the hiddenness of tendencies in any critique toward its own institutionalization, tendencies that can go undetected so long as the oppositional discourse directs attention away from those tendencies in itself and toward the hidden discourses of the targeted institution.

Despite some unfortunate connotations of the word "institution" that arise, perhaps, from its suggestion of a building, of visibility, advanced organization, impersonality, or stability, I prefer it to such alternatives as "community," which is often used by theologians, "profession" (as recently used by Stanley Fish), or "group" (as developed by Fredric Jameson).[13] I prefer it because these other terms, while avoiding some of the misleading connotations of the term "institution," themselves mislead by suggesting political neutrality or informality, as though they were too fluid or underdeveloped to contain their own discourses or duplicities.

Diane Macdonell closely ties discursive to institutional opposition. She points out that "a crucial argument concerning discourse is that meanings are to be found only in the concrete forms of differing social and institutional practices; there can be no meaning in 'language.' "[14] This leads her to conclude that discourses "take shape antagonistically, through the struggles which traverse various institutions"(101). This emphatic connection of discourses with institutions may arise from her dependence on the work of Michel Foucault.

Nancy Fraser points out that Foucault's analysis of the modern power/knowledge regime, by being so thorough and inclusive, creates a problem for locating oppositional sites. In such a totalized situation of institutionalized discourses and their disciplines, there is no place left from which to mount an oppositional discourse. She wants to maintain, for example, some language of human rights as not co-opted by the power/knowledge regime.[15] I would say that the language of totalization, whenever it arises in postmodernist discourses, should be held in check by an equally strong language of difference, opposition, and the tendency toward fragmentation. Such language is available because every discourse or institution, because it is oppositionally generated, implies or anticipates contraries and alternatives to it that can be inferred, articulated, and directed oppositionally to it.

Discourse analysis, therefore, is heavily weighted with political interests, and it does not readily separate discourses from institutional forms of generating power and significance. It does not for several reasons, including the following: institutions have discourses embodied within them; discourses develop their power and significance in relation to and even dependence on the institutions they represent or attack; and discourses that oppose existing institutions contain their own, often concealed, tendencies toward institutionalization.

III

These brief descriptions of conversation analysis, intertextuality, and discourse analysis serve, it is hoped, not only to relate them to and distinguish them from one another but also to trace, from the first (least) to the third (greatest), their influence on this study. This work is carried on in the context provided both by the severance of discourses from those nondiscursive points outside them which often and traditionally have been construed as antedating discourses and providing them their meaning and power, and by such forms of analysis of discourses as these three kinds suggest. What must now be done is to characterize my own approach. Since discourse analysis, as already mentioned, is the most influential for this study, I shall describe the approach taken up in this study in relation primarily to it.

This study conforms to discourse analysis in the following ways. First, it examines theological discourses not in their relation to nondiscursive, antedating points outside of them but in their relation to one another. Second, the argument is not only that theological discourses are oppositionally related to one another but also that their meaning and power are generated by such oppositions. Third, discourses so described cannot be treated in such a way as to separate meaning and power from one another. Finally, theological discourses are always involved, consequently, by way of legitimation or challenge, in social and political structures and dynamics.

This study differs from much discourse analysis, however, in this way: theological discourses are not read as expressions, defenses, or concealments of exclusively or even primarily social, institutional, or political interests. Theological discourses are not only discourses; they are also theological. And this means that the oppositions and conflicts among them, and the power required by and resulting from these interactions, can and should also be traced to their characteristics as theological discourses. This emphasis is not meant to deny the location of theological discourses in social contexts such as institutions, with all their political and economic characteristics. Indeed, theology is itself, as a profession, an institution, one that is in various and complex ways related to other, especially academic and/or ecclesiastical, institutions. This means that theological discourses are never free, open, and innocent.[16] But it also means that theological discourses need not be viewed as disguised forms of political activity. While they can be that, while the unavoidable component of power and authority in theological discourses can, for example, become the means of ambition, privilege, domination, or control, they need not be and generally should not be so interpreted. But tracing and accounting for oppositions and conflicts among theological discourses in theological terms does not necessarily separate theology from its social and political situations either, for, if the meaning and authority of a theological discourse depend upon its supremacy over and discrediting of contrary theological discourses, it cannot achieve its authority and meaning without accruing political power of its own or calling the political supports of an opposing discourse into question. Indeed, it is not only that the political, institutional, and professional components of theological discourses give power to theology but also and just as much that the theological component of those discourses gives power to political, institutional, and professional interests. This study should help show why.

Although the institutional involvement of theological discourses deserves full treatment, nothing approaching that can be given here. However, observations made earlier about the relation of discourses to institutions can be applied to discursive situations created by theologies. Before letting this matter recede, a few more comments can be made.

An important study of the relation of discursive practices to institutions, particularly to professions, is provided by Stanley Fish. His emphasis is on the literary and legal professions as institutions that contain and support interpretive acts. He construes a profession as a matrix of mostly tacit beliefs and directives as to what will stand as a legitimate interpretation of a literary or of a legal text. "Profession" stands as a more visible and specific synonym for what in his earlier work Fish referred to as interpretive communities. The effort of Fish to locate scholarship and knowledge in an institutionalized and therefore also political situation is fruitful. He is able to identify anti-institutionalism or antiprofessionalism in literary studies, for example, as essentialism or idealism. I agree. But it should be noted that Fish presses his discussion of professions to balance what is also of great importance for him, namely, the indeterminancy of texts. Professions, with their tacit boundaries, engrained assumptions, and continuities of practice, stabilize the interpretive situation and keep texts from meaning everything or anything.[17]

My understanding of the relation of theologies to the institution of the profession turns, in contrast to Fish, toward differences and conflicts rather than commonality and agreement, differences that produce irreconcilable interpretations of texts as well as nonnegotiable assumptions as to which texts are more important than others and what in a text counts most. Fish wants to stabilize interpretation by means of the continuity and determinations of practice in order to compensate for the discontinuities and indeterminacy he attributes to texts. Correspondingly, my emphasis on the conflicts among theological discourses, indeed on the dependence upon difference and conflict for the generation of meaning and power, implies an understanding of texts as more determined than he takes them to be. In the Conclusion to this study, when I discuss the culture or language of scripture and belief, I shall have a better occasion to say why a text that a person can and does interpret is not apart from that person and indeterminate but is already, before the interpretation, a part of the practice, already related to assumptions and beliefs.

Furthermore, Fish is more sanguine than I tend to be about institutions and professions. While I am not antiprofessional in the way those he attacks as essentialist are, I am also more uneasy than Fish seems to be about the duplicity of discourses that are implied by or embedded in professions or institutions. This duplicity prevents me from the sort of vigorous proprofessionalism that marks Fish's discussion. Indeed, his position ends, it seems to me, in voice warranting. Discourses seem to derive their significance and authority from the professional identity of their voices, and those who have done particularly well in their professions, who have supremacy within that structure of power, ought particularly, he argues, to be heeded.[18]

Finally, force for Fish is restricted to such uses as the force of an argument or the force of one's convictions. As he says, "Force is simply a (pejorative) name for the thrust or assertion of some point of view . . . another name for what follows naturally from conviction" (521). I think that this use of "force" tends to tie it too closely to the "meaning" or "significance" of discourse and to prevent force from attaching itself to more easily recognizable political interests such as ambition, domination, and control. While I do not trace the potentials and implications of power in theological discourses to their institutional and other political sources and consequences, I also do not want to mitigate those aspects by confining them to and taming them by the theological meanings of those discourses.

The relation of theologies to institutions is complicated, I want also to point out, because the institution in which a theologian works can be different from a profession in that the institution can have been a place of nurture and training for the theologian from birth. In this regard theology as a profession seems unique. Theologians are often closely and deeply identified with ecclesiastical institutions, and their professional or vocational identities are often theologically construed. Many theologians are subjects of their institutions as few other professionals are of theirs. This results in peculiar obligations and consequences for identity, and one of the reasons why theological conflicts can be so virulent is the lack of distance between the theologian's personal and professional identities. Personal, institutional, and theological factors and interests are interconnected. It may also mean that theologians may retain affiliations even when theological practices have distanced them from ecclesiastical identification. Disaffiliation may require a distancing not only from an institution but also from one's youth, nurture, and internalized culture.

Another point that should be made is that Christian churches, no less than other institutions, establish their identities, their power and meaning, by means of differences from and opposition to other churches, other religious institutions, and secular institutions in the society. As William A. Christian puts it, "to maintain its own identity a religious community has to define its stance toward alien patterns of life."[19] This oppositional mode of identity is due in great part to the fact that churches are institutionalized discourses, too. Moreover, strategies of differentiation are necessary not only to the maintenance of identity but to its origination. Churches from root to branch are involved in dynamics of difference and opposition to one another. The relations among Protestant churches, between Protestants and Catholics, between Christian institutions and Jewish, and between any of the above and the surrounding society form an almost bewildering matrix of relationships that include continuities and differences, dependencies and conflicts.

Finally, it should be noted that some theological discourses deny institutional identification and, as Reinhold Niebuhr made clear, hold a rather powerful position because they can appear to be themselves tied to a transcendent perspective and free from institutional determination.[20] This putative freedom of some theological discourses from institutional ties and obligations—I say "some" because not all theological discourses can, by virtue of their basic beliefs, claim to be so freed—gives such theological critiques of institutions great power. But all theological discourses have institutional dependencies and locations, and all theological critiques contain some incipient suggestions concerning social and political, or institutional, interests and arrangements.

However, a great deal of theological justification is given today to critique of and active opposition to institutions. While the legitimacy granted by churches and their languages has in the past and perhaps still in the present been partial to existing institutions—the state, the social order, the family, etc.—today large measures of legitimacy are generated theologically for discourses arrayed not in the defense of such institutions but in their critique. What must be borne in mind, when such legitimacy is granted, is that discourses that oppose existing institutions and their embodied discourses carry within themselves their own implied or incipient institutionalization. While their spokespersons may deny such factors or actually be unconscious of them, those ingredients can and perhaps should be brought to the surface. I do not mean that a discourse that stands opposed to an institution needs, in order to be taken seriously, a fully developed plan for an institution with which to replace the one under attack. I mean, rather, that the oppositional discourse should be interrogated as to the tendencies for its own institutionalization that it carries, including alternative institutions already in existence that it may be serving or institutions in the past that it may be attempting to resuscitate. Theological approval of an oppositional discourse also means approval of the institutionalization that such a discourse carries implicitly within itself. Anyone who has participated in anti-institutional groups and associations will know how well defined an implicit institution can become, how strong the insider/outsider designation, how de rigueur a specific language, and how rigid the standards of admission or orthodoxy. Here I would agree with Stanley Fish; anti-institutionalism and antiprofessionalism in discourse analysis and cultural theory can often be traced to essentialism. I would add that anti-institutionalism and antiprofessionalism serve to conceal the institutional and professional designs and ambitions latent in an oppositional discourse.

2

Theological Discourses and Oppositional Relations

Now that the presuppositions, strategies, and implications of discourse analysis have, however briefly, been sketched, the relation of this kind of analysis to theological studies can be introduced. I shall do this, first, by returning to a question already broached, namely, whether the severance of discourses from their putative or traditional sources of authority and significance threatens theology with invalidation. Next, I shall contrast my treatment of the consequences of postmodernist contexts for theology with two highly visible and consequential studies of a similar kind. Finally, I shall discuss other ways in which and reasons why theologies differ from one another that, while important, lie outside the purview of this work.

I

Discourse analysis, as I noted earlier, attempts, first of all, to free discourses from their dependent and secondary relations to a world apart to which they refer; it denies that entities and events can be detached from the discourses that identify, interpret, and evaluate them. This program or assumption has marked much twentieth-century theory beginning at least with Ferdinand de Saussure, and it reaches one of its fullest expressions and celebrations in Richard Rorty's *Philosophy and the Mirror of Nature.* Rorty writes against the notion that philosophy is a theory of representation and that philosophy distinguishes discourses as to their ability to represent reality well. He follows William James, for whom the norm of "accurate representation of reality" is displaced by the norm "what is better for us to believe." Rorty judges the norm "accurate representation of reality" to be an *a posteriori* justification of beliefs.[1] This means that certainty, instead of arising from a relation between a mind and an object, arises by agreement among interlocutors; "nothing counts as justification unless by reference to what we already accept, and . . . there is no way to get outside our beliefs and our language so as to find some test other than coherence" (178). Rorty turns from the quest for certainty, locates the intellectual life in belief, and identifies the goal of philosophy as a quest for understanding. This requires the exchange of certainty, of brute facts as a common ground, for manifestations of unity that mutual interests and goals, or social and civil ties, provide. The honorific adjective "objective" is reserved for propositions that have a high degree of acceptability among inquirers. The goal of philosophy is edification, self and community building. Richard Bernstein, who pursues an argument similar to Rorty's, summarizes Rorty's project like this:

> It means taking conversation seriously (and playfully), without thinking that the only type of conversation that is important is the type that aspires to put an end to conversation by reaching some sort of "rational consensus," or that all conversation is to be construed as a disguised form of inquiry about the "truth." It means not being fooled into thinking that there is or must be something more fundamental than the contingent social practices that have been worked out in the course of history, that we

> can find some sort of foundation or metaphysical comfort for our human projects.[2]

The task of philosophy is principally critical, then; that is, it works to keep the human "conversation" going, to resist and to rout all temptations and threats to end it.

The intellectual and cultural milieu nominated as postmodernist rests on nothing so much as on this removal of discourse from its secondary, subservient position in relation to the world of referents and granting to language and discourse a primary and determining position. Both structuralist and poststructuralist modes of thought depend on this move, the latter, in ways already suggested, more than the former. The meaning effects of language and discourse are taken to depend not first of all on that to which reference is made but on the force of discourse, a force generated, among other ways, by the constitution of referents and their authority. The general assumption characteristic of this entire milieu is that the objects of discourse, that to which discourses refer, are dependent for their standing and authority on the discourse.

This assumption of or strategy for discourse analysis may at first seem threatening to theological discourses, since it appears to dissolve their truth claims and explicit concerns. Theological language, one may assume, has nothing more important for its projects than faithful articulations about that to which it refers, that which it claims to be the case, and it refers to certainties beyond itself, to which it defers and which it tries to protect. To view the referential effects of theological discourses as constituted by the discourses themselves appears to make theology a grand self-deception, concealing its actual standing concerning that of which it speaks from both its spokespersons and its hearers. However, this observation about the way discourses constitute and validate their objects or referents and then treat them as the causes of the discourse's authority need not be (and seems not to have been) disconcerting for theology. For none of the matters that can be designated as theological starting points, referents, or objects could be construed as entities or events in any straightforward way. Whether one takes that object or starting point to be God, the relations of the divine to the human in some form or event, or the moral and spiritual needs and potentials of people, one does not deal with matters that are accessible apart from the languages that have designated them. Indeed, it seems that a principal role of theological discourse is often to distinguish its "objects" from the specificities of referents that the reader is likely to have in mind.

Furthermore, theology in the modern period was thrown on the defensive by the culture of certainty about facts and reality, or events and entities, and modern theologies that tried to establish their own objective certainties did not do so without cost and met with questionable success. Rather than threatened by the antifoundationalism of the postmodernist situation, theology, to some degree, appears to be "normalized." What can be seen as always true of theology—namely, that it serves to constitute that of which it speaks—can now be seen as true of all discourses, including scientific, historical, and philosophical projects. Rather than assume that other discourses are stabilized by their solid referents, while theological discourses are destabilized by the elusive and unusual status of that to which they refer, it can be assumed that all discourses, no matter how directed toward data and facts they appear to be, are also always constituting and validating their objects and not serving them as though facts and reality, or events and entities, were authoritatively there in some immediately available way. This does not mean that since all discourses constitute their objects and their norms for speaking accurately or adequately about them, any discourse has as much chance as any other of appearing credible or useful no matter what it claims to report or depict. This is because we are always in some social/cultural situation, some discursive context, that will tend to make the "referents" of some discourses appear normal and even unquestionable and others to be dubious.[3] The situation that theological discourses are in nowadays is not so much that they are put in an awkward position by discourses that derive their power and significance differently but that the power and significance of theological discourses has been relegated to particular institutions or to the social periphery, particularly the private lives of people. Appropriate tactics in this situation might be, then, to point out that the assumptions and claims constituted by other discourses are not so certain in standing or value as they appear to be, to point out that other discourses are based on beliefs as to what is important, normative, and valuable, and to challenge the separation of private and public that in our culture is so easy to make. An important "theological" task, then, is discourse analysis that undermines the putative grounding claimed by other discourses in facts, that identifies the role of belief in all discourses, and that resists an easy and fixed distinction between the private and the public spheres or Romantic and Pragmatic impulses.[4]

A second assumption of discourse analysis is that discourses do not carry validating stamps pressed on them by sponsoring minds or subjects. It is not as though the truth or authority of a discourse is imparted to it by the strength or purity of rationality, the feelings of the speaker, or the speaker's moral character. Rather, the discourse itself warrants the voice that sponsors it. One of the meaning effects of any discourse is to give authority to its speaker. Theories of reason, integrity, sincerity, indeed theories of the entire "inner world," it has been recently argued (with psychological theories especially targeted), are to be taken primarily as strategies designed to grant authority to the discourse by warranting its voice and grounding it in its subject.[5] This characteristic of discourses—that they warrant their sponsoring voices—is true whether appeals for authority are made to universal rules of logic, feelings, moral worth, experience, gender, tradition, community, disinterestedness, imagination, office, or learning. All discourses carry within them and constitute the reasons why the hearer is asked to take what the discourse affirms as valid because of the authority that resides in the speaker or because of the relation of the discourse to some sort of prior "inner world." This skepticism of discourse analysis—that the validity of discourses is not grounded in some aspect of the inner world and that this inner world is constituted and validated by the discourse in order to give warrant to its source or voice—undercuts the authority not only of the author as originator, as preexisting the discourse, but also institutions that rest heavily on such assumptions, such as professional, religious, or educational institutions that fortify their positions by constituting and certifying authorities. For discourse analysis, the authority of the source or subject is created by the discourse, and source or subject does not possess authority apart from discourse, as though, for example, reason could be independently elevated to a position from which discourses could be judged to flow, carrying with them reason's validity and authority. The subject is both constituted and warranted by the discourse. One strategy of discourse analysis is to discover terms in a discourse that have been deployed to erect criteria by which the speaker, voice, subject, or source will be taken as reliable and the discourse, consequently, as true.

The warranting of voice is no less true of theological discourses. They deal in terms that constitute the authority not only of the object but also of the subject, source, or sponsor. The notion that discourse is designed to grant authority to source, subject, or voice also seems at first to threaten theology because of the importance so often placed by theology on its source or voice, on revelation, on the institution or community, on faith, or on religious experience. But, again, this exchange need not be (and seems not to have been) troubling for theology, since none of these "authorities," or forms and occasions of warrant, are generally taken as already there in some unproblematic way and requiring neither construction nor defense. Theologies have not been able to assume the widely accepted authority of their sources as have philosophical, scientific, or historical discourses. An important "theological" task, therefore, is to point out that all discourses, not only theological, give standing to their sponsors and validate their putative sources, doing so in relation to beliefs as to what grants authority, credibility, and normativeness to discourses. This constitutes a stronger move than the attempt to mimic other discourses, to contend that the authority or validity of a theological discourse derives from something that antedates the discourse—revelation, the Church, the Christian community, faith, or religious experience. Such a move forces these "sources" of theology to compete with other validating sources such as reason, disinterestedness, or universal rules of formal logic for authority. Postmodernist contexts put the "faith and reason" contrast in an entirely new and, it seems to me, more productive situation.

In this new situation, however, theological appeals to "Church," "revelation," the "Christian community," and faith as starting points free from discourses that constitute and validate them cannot be made. Theological discourses that try to warrant voice or source by appeals to its authority, when they themselves constitute that authority, pretend that sponsor or origin validates discourse, and discourse analysis will question or discredit that move. But theologians, when locked in conflicts between faith and reason, religion and science, or church and university, play games they probably cannot win and certainly need not initiate. A more productive move would be to accept the self-warranting of theological discourses and to identify the ground of voice warranting in other discourses as belief.

Discourse analysis, finally, must also be distinguished from structuralism and semiotics, although such modes of thought and analysis are similar to discourse analysis by also opposing the authority of the referent and of the author. They do so by referring to language and sign systems that determine meaning. Structuralist modes of analysis, beginning at least with de Saussure, not only turned discourse away from the stabilizing world of the referent and to the interplay of language itself but also placed the generating source of meaning not in the speaker but in *langue* or sign systems. *Parole* is really a performance on an already existing repertoire of linguistic possibilities. Discourse analysis, while in agreement at several points with structuralism and semiotics, turns away from them for two reasons, or in two ways.

Structuralist and semiotic theories, in their claims concerning something that lies outside of or antecedent to the discursive situation, grant putative externality to language. Instead of placing emphasis on the structures and dynamics of rationality or some other aspect of the interior life, emphasis is placed by structuralist and semiotic theories on linguistic or sign systems that have a supposedly external existence. But as John Carlos Rowe argues convincingly, such theories of language, deep structures, and sign systems really represent an externalizing of something construed previously as internal.[6] The change is from the language of mind or forms to the language of structure or system, and Rowe sees this as an exchange of Kantian or neo-Kantian terms for a language about language or sign systems. Actually, theories about language, sign systems, or structures replace both the language of nature and the language of mind, retaining the externality of "nature" (by presenting language as external to mind) and the internality of "mind" (by presenting language as generative of meaning). It can be said, therefore, that structuralist and semiotic theories no less than appeals to the certainty of fact, on the one hand, or the authority of mind or ideas, on the other, are discourses that constitute what appear to be their sources and defer to those constructs in order to conceal the actual situation, namely that the systems and structures that supposedly produce and grant significance to discourses are actually produced and projected by them. As much as to referent or to voice, discourse analysis cuts the ties of discourses to putative structures and systems that are thought to antedate, sponsor, and stabilize discourses.

Secondly, discourse analysis is critical of the political implications in the latent humanism that can be detected in structuralism. As Diane Macdonell puts it, discourse analysis "has rejected the belief that a single and general system lies behind all discourses."[7] She goes on to clarify why: "Saussure's linguistics used a humanist notion of society, and supposed that anything social was homogeneous and held in common by everyone" (11). Macdonell attributes this move to a political interest, namely, the desire to conceal or to undercut class differences and struggles behind a theory of a common *langue.*

Severing the ties of discourses from supposedly pre-existent structures or systems may appear less threatening to theology than the other two cuts. Projected appeals of theological discourses to systems, structures, or patterns is not so pervasive as are theories or assumptions in theology about the primacy of that to which theological discourses refer or the authority of their sponsoring sources. However, apologies for Christian theology based on social and psychological systems and structures, whether of myths and symbols, of recurring patterns of religious life postulated by phenomenologists of religion, or of a theory of archetypes by which the unconscious life of individuals or of societies is organized, are common. Whether this takes the ontological form of the language of depth as with Paul Tillich or the Jungian interests of a David L. Miller, whether influenced by Rudolf Otto, Mircea Eliade, or Joseph Campbell, the theological enterprise has been often located in relation to systems, structures, or patterns beneath or behind discourses that stabilize, deepen, organize, or validate them. What is so appealing in such moves is the establishment of Christian theology not only on something universally human—the actual relation or need for relation to an underlying system, structure, or pattern—but on something natural and ontological—the basic structure of the unconscious, the participation of people in the natural order and cycles of life, or the immediate identification of the human mind with the moment of beginnings, in its need for temporal orientation, and with the center, in its need for spatial orientation. Such theological discourses have, as both their source and their object, systems, structures, and patterns that the discourses themselves establish and then claim to be independent and primary. But here again theology need not be embarrassed, as though it alone constituted and validated its objects and authority. The patterns and structures to which psychology and sociology are attentive are no differently derived.

The assumption of this study is that theological discourses, like all discourses, by directing attention to their referents, to their sponsors, or to antedating structures, codes, or patterns, conceal their dependence on belief and on the dynamics by which their power and meaning actually and primarily are produced, namely, by oppositional relations within and among them due to differing beliefs. The purpose of this study is so to clarify the crucial belief differences and the dynamics of opposition those differences create among theologies that another way of reading theologies becomes both warranted in theory and fruitful in practice.

II

Of course, this study does not represent the first attempt to apply postmodernist interests to theological studies. Among previous attempts, two particularly stand out. These prominent texts, which deal with theology in a postmodernist context, although published in the same year, fail adequately, it seems to me, to clarify the consequences for theology of that context, because they employ postmodernist interests to promote already existing theological goals and because they conceal the oppositional relations that theological discourses both hold to one another and require. I refer to George A. Lindbeck's *The Nature of Doctrine* and Mark C. Taylor's *Erring*. However influential they have been, these texts do not provide new ways of reading theologies. Rather, they attempt to validate traditional, or at least recognizable, theological interests with the help of postmodernist assumptions.

The Nature of Doctrine assumes much of the theory that I have briefly described. Lindbeck takes structuralist and poststructuralist modes of thought as defining the limits or linguistic conditions within or under which theology must be done. But the reason why he so readily adopts these modes of thought is that they seem to disqualify from serious consideration theologies that one could generally label as "liberal," theologies that Lindbeck dislikes. Such theologies, he argues, are wedded to modernist modes of thought; they postulate universals and appeal to experience as though to something secure and shared. This foundationalism becomes untenable in a poststructuralist situation, and Lindbeck proposes that doctrines be taken, instead, in a "cultural, linguistic" way, that is, as communally located rules directing the Christian community's discourses, attitudes, and actions.

Lindbeck realizes that by endorsing postmodernist assumptions the referential force of doctrines also is called into question. But this more objectivist consequence he does not pursue as he does the subjectivist, the discrediting of what he calls "experiential-expressive" theories of doctrine. He assures his readers that "a religion can be interpreted as possibly containing ontologically true affirmations, not only in cognitivist theories but also in cultural-linguistic ones. There is nothing in the cultural-linguistic approach that requires the rejection . . . of the epistemological realism and correspondence theory of truth [embedded in the theological tradition]."[8] In other words, Lindbeck's project of severing religious doctrines from ties to subjective sources and referents and of locating them in the life of the Christian community is also a project to protect and preserve the objectivist or referential standing or thrust of doctrine.

This unbalanced or incomplete use of postmodernist discourses, it seems to me, is questionable. What goes for the subjectivist side goes for the objectivist, too. To employ postmodernist modes of thought is to cut discourses from the security and stability of both poles. Never mind, for now, that some of the people, such as Eliade, whom he treats as subjectivists are actually objectivists and that it is a certain kind of objectivism he wants to preserve; Lindbeck is using postmodernist modes of thought selectively, for postmodernism makes more cuts and changes than he admits.

It is also possible to read Lindbeck as a structuralist of sorts, one who posits doctrines as rules or directives that shape the way the Christian community can and does construe reality and carry on its life. It appears that, as in the structural semantics of A. J. Greimas, doctrines operate beneath language, directing its configurations the way a magnet determines the configurations of iron fillings on a surface.[9] It is not altogether clear if it is the Christian community, as a historically or socially identifiable and particular group, or some structure shaping the community from beneath that gives rise to doctrine. In any case, Christian discourses find their stability and authority in something claimed to antedate them. Such a move is questionable in the present context.

Finally, Lindbeck is engaged in voice warranting. His theology projects as primary what it itself constitutes, namely, "the Christian Community" as real and authoritative. Moreover, he imputes to this construct a unity and universality that one does not find when one looks at various, competing, and often disputing Christian communities. It is surprising that Lindbeck can assume such a source or voice when the situation constituted by Christian communities is one of difference and opposition. In order to warrant his discourse Lindbeck simply posits a unity where primarily diversity and difference occur.

Although he employs postmodernist modes of analysis, Lindbeck retains crucial ingredients of objectivism, voice warranting or subjectivism, and structuralism. All of these ingredients serve his theology to give it its meaning and authority. Its principal objective is the Church identified as Christian community and projected as generative of doctrine, a reality whose unique significance and authority must be protected from the generalizing and compromising consequences of "experiential-expressive" theologies. "Cultural-linguistic" and other poststructuralist terms are used to establish a traditional ecclesiological interest: the Church as "one, holy, universal, and apostolic."

Mark Taylor's *Erring* makes fuller use of and draws more radical conclusions from the situation that postmodernism appears to create for theology.[10] Taylor carries on his critique more from a deconstructive perspective than Lindbeck. Rather than use postmodernist theory to defend the separateness of the Church and the doctrines it sponsors from their nonchurch environments, Taylor uses mainly Derrida to attack the possibility of separateness and identity. He posits an undifferentiated plain where distinctions and particularities are dissolved and dismembered.

Taylor shares with Lindbeck a denunciation of the modernist, humanist project. He claims that its culmination was the announcement of God's death and the deification of humans. The self becomes absolute and the human a transcendental signified, a stable, originating, and culminating point of reference that gives language meaning, constancy, and reliability.

Taylor does not posit God as the transcendental signified. Rather, he dismantles traditional Christianity and its doctrines along with Western humanism. To do this he uses what have become standard deconstructive points: That the signified is always also a signifier, that no text, system, or structure has a center, that all boundaries are permeable and all meaning relational, that the world to which we refer is always already textualized, and that time is a passage from future into past without a stable present. Referents are actually only names for gathered attributes that we mistakenly take as unified and constant. His key word is "writing," and he means by it a vast, boundless, leveled terrain of uncentered, mutually canceling, and interdependent meanings from which human life is inseparable and upon which humans hopelessly wander.

Taylor uses this postmodernist tack as preliminary to his theological project, which is to identify "writing" as the divine milieu, the locus of a continual process of incarnation. This incarnation is radically kenotic, for the "word" becomes not flesh but script, and writing is the radical other of "word" as logos or coherence. Taylor posits writing and the human state of homelessness as a divine milieu that turns that bleak terrain into a playing field and even into a vast home.

Although the deconstructive and theological sides of Taylor's project are inseparable from one another, I shall comment on them separately. Concerning the deconstructive part, first: Taylor's emphasis on a total terrain that we all, despite our differences, share, conceals the differences, especially social and political differences, between people that grant privileges and powers to some and not to others. His discounting of such differences leaves the analyst helpless in dealing with the problem of protected and concealed inequalities. Secondly, Taylor, even more than Derrida, I think, discounts present time. When present time is lost, as it is in this text, time is lost, too. There is something terribly spatial and atemporal about the picture Taylor paints. This is because future and past have both been textualized and, as a result, spatialized. Present time, while it seems to be no part of time at all, is indispensable to time, strange as that may seem. By removing it, Taylor removes temporality from his depiction. This serves the quite static situation he wants to project, and a dehistoricized as well as depoliticized human situation is the result.

Concerning his theological point: on the other side of the deconstructive effort, Taylor posits writing as the divine milieu. This point depends for its intelligibility on a specific group of "intertexts" that are being granted, however unconsciously, a position of centrality, "intertexts" that stress the presence of God not in power but in weakness, not in the center but at the fringes, not in self-assertion but in anonymity, not in grasping but in emptying. Taylor's implied canon includes Paul on weakness and foolishness and on the incarnation in Philippians 2, the tradition of Christian asceticism, Luther on humility, Kierkegaard on sacrifice and Bonhoeffer on discipleship (to name only a few). True, Taylor's point is extreme, but his text depends on and imputes authority to texts already there that support it. Taylor's text takes a place on the terrain of writing by gathering intertexts upon which the identity of his theology depends. Like Lindbeck, he uses postmodernist modes of thought to support a traditional, although extreme, theological project. For this reason, it seems to me, his work does not alter the theological enterprise, however dependent on postmodernist themes and radical in his application of them to many Christian interests he may be.

These texts by Lindbeck and Taylor, although apparently different from one another, are alike in several ways: they appeared together, have been much commented upon, attack liberalism and humanism, and use postmodernist modes of analysis to make traditional theological points. More important for this study, however, is that they both present theology as a nonoppositional kind of discourse. Lindbeck does this by isolating the Christian community as a single, self-enclosed, and generative reality determined by its own particular and coherent rules. Taylor does this by dissolving all differences into a vast and common field of crisscrossing and mutually canceling meanings. As a consequence, both obscure what I take to be the major consequence of postmodernism for theology by concealing the dependence of theological discourses on one another and on their differences from one another for their force and meaning. I take this as a particularly important and challenging point to make about theological discourses. It is not so much a negative point—that theological discourses are not to be taken first of all in terms of their referents, their sources, or structures and systems, which are derived from and dependent on the discourses themselves—as a positive point concerning what theological discourses are primarily about. In a word, they are primarily about their own internal dynamics in relation to those of theologies with which they differ.

III

Before going on to delineate the ways in which and the reasons why theological discourses depend upon their differences from and oppositions to one another, it is necessary to discuss kinds of and reasons for theological difference and opposition that I shall *not* be treating. There are three other kinds or sources of differences or conflicts that should be mentioned both because of their importance and because of their distinction from the kinds I shall be considering.

Christians differ from one another, first of all, in ways determined by historical, social, and cultural factors. Differences of this kind are synchronically available in denominationalism. It becomes possible to place denominations in rough relation to cultural and class differences.[11] Theological distinctions available in denominationalism, although more difficult to establish, can be traced because ecclesiastical institutions have theological discourses inscribed or embodied in them and are hospitable to some and antagonistic to other theologies. The principal point to be kept in mind is that culture and class, as Pierre Bourdieu points out, are closely related, and tastes, along with rationale for them, are to be traced not only to historical factors but also to social classes and their differences or distinctions.[12] The identity-granting capacity of class is not confined to such matters as preferences in clothing, food, or sports. It also has moral and even spiritual aspects. For example, upper-class people will think of themselves as morally superior to lower-class people, who will be thought of as lazy and unreliable. But working-class people will think of their own lives as more moral than those of the upper classes, because people in their own class are, in their view, more concerned for and caring toward one another, harder workers, more appreciative of what they have, and more honest, direct, or less artificial than those above them. If this is so—and I find Bourdieu persuasive—then there are likely to be theological differences along the lines of social and economic distinctions, forms of theological identity that would appear if the sociological data were gathered in the painstaking way Bourdieu gathered the material for his conclusions about the economic/social bases of cultural differences in France.

A second reason why Christians differ from one another has recently been described by Stephen Sykes.[13] He points out that differences, disagreements, and conflicts were inherent to the Christian tradition from the very beginning. They arose from and are contained in the complexity of the material—the life of Jesus and of the early Church—and its underdetermined character. That is, from the outset there were many differing points to be stressed and no overriding set of norms that determined how the many differing emphases were to be resolved and agreement achieved. Texts concerning Jesus, for example, contain too much variety and inherent ambiguity to assure that only one, all-inclusive interpretation, rather than many conflicting ones, would arise. "Controversy is simply unavoidable," he concludes (23). Differences and conflicts are inevitable because of the complexities of the discourses concerning Jesus, because of the indeterminacy of Christian texts, and because Christianity was and is "multifaceted" (26). Christianity is unsettled theologically not only because Christians emphasize various facets of the faith but also because these emphases vary according to changing historical circumstances. One can add to this last point of Sykes what in postmodernist hermeneutics is seen more generally and strongly to be the case, namely, the indeterminacy of texts and the interpretation of texts as always affected by assumptions and beliefs in the historically conditioned situations, what Stanley Fish calls "interpretive communities," in which the readings take place.[14] Differences in readings are not negotiable by appeals to the text, not only because the text causes these differing readings, as Sykes emphasizes, but also because different interests or expectations are brought to the text by readers in various circumstances, differences that produce varying readings. Frank Kermode's work can also be used to amplify the point of Sykes because Kermode stresses the inherent ambiguities of Christian Scripture, especially the Gospel of Mark. One characteristic of Scripture, for Kermode, is its ability to give rise to various readings and to seem inexhaustible in the meanings it contains. There are, he contends, strategies that grant a text this potential.[15] All of these ways of putting the issue help demonstrate that Christians differ from one another because of the complex and elusive material to which they respond, the indeterminacy of texts, and the various circumstances that condition the interpretations of the texts.

Christians differ from one another, thirdly, because of the possibility, perhaps the necessity, of actualizing three ways of expressing or characterizing the life of faith. Sykes calls these three ways "theatres" of interest—"thought, word, and deed." He quotes John Henry Newman: "Christianity is dogmatical, devotional, practical all at once."[16] I think that this distinction of arenas, forms of expression, or "theatres" of interest is even more important than Sykes allows.

A major source of disagreement among Christians can be exposed by distinguishing emphases on hand, heart, and head from one another. Christians will differ as to which of the three should be dominant, even though they may agree that all three are appropriate or even necessary forms of Christian interest. Moreover, it would be possible, I believe, to determine which of the three is dominant for a particular Christian even though he or she may not want to choose one of them as more important than the others. This means that there are categories of Christians identifiable as to which of the three is most important—what one thinks and professes, what one does in daily life, or what one feels in the heart.

Pietism, for example, needs to be defined in large measure as an emphasis on "heart," on feeling, and as a reaction to the "heady" orientations of Protestant scholasticism or the formalism of Christian actions in state church situations. Pietism, revivalism, and evangelicalism, however different from one another they may be, are similar to one another in this regard.

An important source of difference, even tension, between or among Christians today concerns the kind of primacy that should be given to "hand," especially in relation to an emphasis on "head," or on theology. A privileging of social and political concerns and actions, of "praxis" over doctrine, characterizes many contemporary, especially liberation, theologies. In this situation theology is subordinated to a rationale for or a directive toward social and political action that has as its goal primarily to subvert oppressive structures and to come to the aid of the oppressed—the poor, minorities, or women. So, for example, Nicholas Lash, with explicit references to Marx and Lenin, remarks that "unless we risk seeking responsibly to live and act in the world, any theoretical 'purchase' that we imagine ourselves to have upon reality is fragile and suspect." "The Christian," he goes on to say, "must prove the truth, i.e. the reality and power, the this-sidedness of his believing in practice."[17] Frederick Herzog entitles his book *God-Walk: Liberation Shaping Dogmatics* to clarify his priorities in opposition to the title of John Macquarrie's *God-Talk* (1967). "Some dogmatics texts," says Herzog in reference to his subtitle, "still begin from the premise that theory provides guidelines for walking in the world—for action. The project of *liberation shaping dogmatics,* by contrast, is premised on the inescapably conflictual context where praxis precedes theory. Dogmatics now is shown to arise out of God-walk. Praxis gives rise to thought."[18] This priority, even normative, determinative status, given to action, particularly political and social action, creates a climate in which an orientation dominated by "head" rather than "hand," an orientation determined primarily by theology, that is, is put on the defensive and itself termed a political and social position, one, that is, which conceals its intention to protect the political, social, and economic status quo.

Although among the theological examples that will be examined fairly closely later on there is one liberation theologian, I have chosen the work of people who do theology more for its own sake than as a justification or imperative toward social and political action. Even for Leonardo Boff, it seems to me, acts directed toward liberation arise from an already existing theology, a theology that can effect other appropriate responses or results as well.

The tension created within theological circles today by the differing directions and priorities that flow from an emphasis on "hand" rather than "head" has more implications for this study than the selection of theologies as examples. Discourse analysis, for reasons I already have suggested, presupposes understandings of language that not only break down the distinctions between knowledge and power or language and political interests but tend to privilege matters of power and politics. My position through all of this has been to affirm, first, that force and meaning are always involved with one another. This involvement always ties theologies to political implications, possibilities, and consequences, and theologians need to be more aware than they may at times be of the actual and potential relations of their discourses to institutional and other political interests. Secondly, I also want to affirm that the force of theological discourses is not merely political but is also theological, produced, that is, by the dynamics of theological differences. The force and meaning of theological discourses should not be interpreted as simply disguised ways of securing, legitimating, or challenging political or social power.

By selecting theologies that place "head" over "hand" and "heart," I may appear to exclude or at least discount the other two "theatres" of interest. I would say that all three are always there, although the one "theatre" will be emphasized, and in this case it is the "head" or theological. But I do not discredit, by this choice of dominant, the other two kinds of emphasis. All three are, it seems to me, equally valid and necessary, and no one of the three is a more legitimate dominant than either or both of the other two. The "head" orientation of this study does not imply that it always is or should be the dominant, although it does imply that this interest or "theatre" provides as legitimate a dominant as either "heart" or "hand." Nor do I believe that this dominant allows a kind of idealism to slip in by the rear door. Beliefs and ideas do not precede or transcend actions and experiences; they are always tied to them, as they are as well to convictions and emotions. All three are always present and finally not separable from one another. But there are not only relations of dependence and influence of the three on one another; there are also tensions among them. These are resolved when one dominates the other two; indeed, it seems almost inevitable that one of them will. Problems arise when that dominant is taken as permanent and universal, the legitimacy of the other orientations denied, and an independence of the dominant from the others declared. All of these distortions are very much a part of the way we think about language and thought in our culture, and emphasis on the other theaters or the possibilities for dominance in the other factors is a necessary and salutary response to distortions. It solves nothing to make today the sort of claims for the primacy of "hand" that have mistakenly and with distorting consequences been made during the modern period for the absolute dominance of "head" or "heart."

There are, then, three ways in which or reasons why Christians differ from one another, ways that are not treated by this study. Christians find themselves in differing conditions, conditions historically, socially, politically, and culturally created or determined, which give rise to differences among them. In addition, Christianity's sources and its principal texts are complicated and supportive of differing and varying emphases and interpretations. Finally, there are the differences that arise when Christians emphasize, as they inevitably will do, one of the three "theatres" of Christian interest—actions, feelings, or reflection.

In this study I turn attention to another way by which Christians are bound to differ from one another. It has to do with the more limited area of theological articulation, with theological discourses. What I want to point out is that these discourses are governed by dynamics that make difference and conflict both inevitable and causal. These differences are not incidental, avoidable, or in any way secondary in theological discourses; they are integral to their very life. Indeed, theological discourses do not fully actualize their potential power and significance unless or until maximum differences mark their relations to theological discourses with which they stand in opposition.

3

The Dynamics of Theological Discourses

A Model

THIS ANALYSIS OF THEOLOGICAL argumentation stresses those moments that cast theological discourses into relations of conflict and thereby generate theological power and significance. These moments also reveal similarities among theological discourses, similarities that allow the analyst to place discourses into groups, to describe the characteristics of each group, and to give each a name. While there are oppositions *within* such groups, oppositions that also contribute to a particular discourse's power and significance, these oppositions seem to be less inevitable and causal than are those that exist *between* or among the groups. I shall include the former but stress the latter.

I

Although Christian theologians talk about many things and often range widely into various other fields of inquiry and thought, they do so in relation to a specific agenda of recurring, even required, interests. They talk about God, the person and work of Jesus Christ, the Church, human nature, especially the evils in human life and how they are overcome, and about the end of human existence or of the world. Scholastic Protestantism put these various topics under six categories: theology, Christology, ecclesiology, anthropology, soteriology and eschatology. This is a useful set of categories, and I shall use them later, subjecting them, however, to another purpose. So, for example, I shall discuss Karl Barth's "theology," that is, his discussion of God, Jürgen Moltmann's "eschatology," his orientation to the future or to last things, Leonardo Boff's "Christology," Hans Küng's "ecclesiology," and the "anthropology" and "soteriology" of a number of American theologians. But I shall subject these topics to another set of interests. For while all of the theologians talk about all of these topics, they do so from differing bases and with predictable results. The topics by themselves do not have determining and conflict-producing effects, and they should not be treated as the originators of the dynamics of theological discourses.

The dynamics of difference arise from the three separable meaning effects produced by all theologies. These meaning effects stand in conflict with one another because any of them can be primary and dominate the other two. In fact, a theological discourse can largely be described as a set of strategies to establish and defend the domination of one of these three meaning effects over the other two.

First, theological language concerning God, heaven, grace, predestination, final judgment, and the like can be grouped together as signifying matters that are contrary to or apart from what participants in the discourse assume to be the world open to human understanding and control. When words such as supernatural, transcendent, or eternal are used it is to these sorts of interests that attention is being drawn. Theologies consider matters postulated as apart from and even contrary to the space and time of human affairs. Humans not only do not but cannot understand or control these matters. Although theologians differ in what they take to be the significance and importance of this language, theology requires it for one of its meaning effects. It is difficult to name these interests without privileging one kind of theological discourse concerning them. So, I will label signifiers of this kind by using a simple sign rather than a descriptive phrase. I will designate them as "x" matters.

A second set of theological signifiers concerns various and particular entities or events in our world that form an identifiable class because in them "x" matters are made available to people. Christian theologians are not interested in "x" matters in the abstract. They relate them to forms, events, or aspects in or of our world that allow people to have some degree of relation with "x" matters. Sometimes the special entities or events are located in the past and people have a relation to them indirectly by reports. Or they can be in the future, and relation to them is available through predictions or precursors. Often the form or occasion is not so distant. Although there are wide variations and differences among theologies depending on what is affirmed to be that form or occasion—Scripture, the Church, the person and work of Jesus, the sacraments, the created order, etc.—all theologies must designate where or how it is possible for people to gain knowledge of, contact with, or participation in "x" matters. I will group signifiers of and interest in such occasions or forms under the letter "y."

A third group of theological signifiers can be distinguished from these two. Theologians also are concerned with the conditions and possibilities of the human world. Generally these interests, while starting with the human, become inclusive of the larger world, not only individuals, society, and culture but also cosmos. Evil, both moral and natural, human potential, cosmology, the nature and meaning of human history, the transformations of personal and social life: interests such as these form a third set of theological signifiers that can be grouped under one heading as "z" matters.

There are two hidden premises in theological argumentation that should be recognized.[1] The first is that all three kinds of signifiers *are always required.* If thought is given, say, to "x" matters without interest shown in their availability to human beings and their consequences for human well-being, such thought is not theological. Or, if there is an interest taken in the moral or spiritual potentials or needs of human beings without relating them to some events or entities in which it is believed a relation to the "transcendent," say, is possible, the discourse is not theological. Theological discourses include signifiers and interests of all three kinds. To put it another way, the task of theological discourses is to set and to argue the relations among one another of these three kinds of signifiers. Discourses, no matter how much they may be directed toward matters of religious or theological interest, are not theological if they lack as their hidden premise that all three of these groups of signifiers must be included in the theology and that the relations between and the consequences for one another that they carry must be declared and maintained.

The second hidden premise in theological discourse is that these three sets of signifiers or interests, while always all present, are not of equal importance. Rather, *one of the three will be more important than and will dominate the other two.* In describing the three sets of signifiers and interests I may have been misleading, for the sequential arrangement suggests some kind of chronological or logical order. It may appear as though "x" matters hold precedence over "y" and "z." That is far from the case. Any one of the three can become the dominant. The two points must be made with equal emphasis: (1) In any theological discourse all three kinds of signifiers will be present; and (2) in any theological discourse one of them will dominate the other two and deform them toward itself.[2] To repeat, all three interests are equally capable of holding that dominating position. When I say that in any particular theological discourse the set of signifiers and interests that dominates the other two will not only subject them but will deform them to itself, I mean that theological argumentation largely establishes its dominant by denying the dominance of the other two kinds of signifiers and by showing why its dominant cancels or absorbs the potential for dominance in the other two.

Keeping these characteristics in mind one can project, then, three kinds of theological discourses. To put the matter as clearly as possible, a diagram can be used.

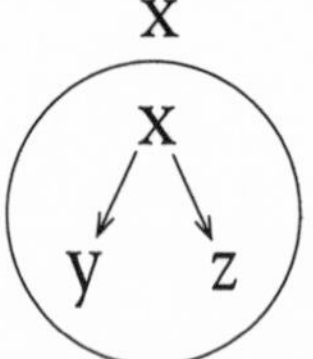

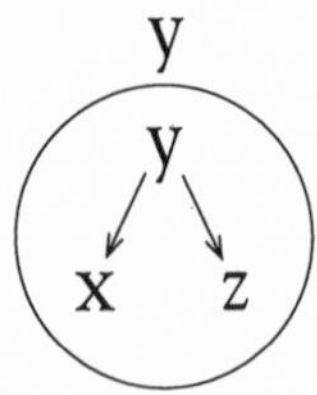

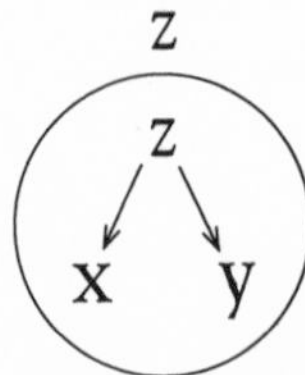

This is a model that describes both continuity and discontinuity in theological work. The continuity arises from the necessary inclusion in theological discourses of all three kinds of language. The discontinuity arises from the difference in dominants. And, since each set of interests is as fully capable of dominating as either of the other two, this discontinuity or difference is bound to appear.

II

The major premise of a particular theological argument concerns its dominant. This premise is not hidden, but it is often not directly defended. This is due to the fact that its assumed primacy implies that there is nothing above the dominant or beneath the starting point that grants it its primacy. Rather, its legitimacy is argued more indirectly, by demonstrating that the other, remaining two sets of signifiers or interests are not, should not, or could not be primary or dominant. The situation in which the primacy or dominance of one of the sets of signifiers is taken as obvious is certainly reinforced by historical and institutional conditions, but such factors should not conceal how important it is for a discourse to assume the primacy of its dominant or starting point and to argue that assumption by discrediting the possibility of either of the two remaining sets of signifiers or interests for holding that position. The "basic belief" of a theological discourse is the belief in the rightful place of its dominant and, consequently, in the subordinate, dependent, or derivative positions of the other two interests or kinds of signifiers.

A person or group for which "x" matters dominate, for example, holds firmly and takes as obvious both that those signifiers serve as the starting point and that all other theological interests must be subservient and shaped by the dominant. The question of whether either the form of availability to the human world of "x" matters or their relation to human needs and potentials should receive equal attention with "x" interests seems, for such people, not even to arise let alone be addressed in a direct way. Those for whom "y" interests are dominant seem also to believe that it is obvious that the arrangement should be so and that what is said about the other interests, about, say, "God" and about "human needs and potentials," is dependent on and derived from the "y" signifiers. And those for whom "z" interests are primary believe that it is perfectly obvious that attention to human needs and potentials, for example, constitutes the first responsibility of Christian theology and that concern about the other two matters is to follow from such interests.

Theological argumentation does not, then, first of all concern such topics as "God," the "presence of Christ in the sacrament," "human sin and restoration," and the like. It concerns the relations of these things to one another, their dominant and subordinate positions. What needs to be argued is the rightness of a particular set of relations. And this is done not so much by arguing for the position of the dominant as by arguing against the potential for dominance that seems to reside in the other two interests. Once that argument is made, the theological task is basically completed and the rest is a matter of elaborating or extending the content and implications of this arrangement.

A theological discourse, then, seen in terms of itself, contains an arrangement or a setting of internal priorities, the subservience of two of its interests to its dominant one. This arrangement is clarified, established, or reinforced, and its implications developed. If such a vast institutionalization of a particular kind of theological discourse has occurred that there is little possibility the assumed dominant will be threatened by the potential for dominance in the subservient interests, little theological activity will occur. Theological argumentation arises as the consequence of a perceived threat to the arrangement posed by the potential for dominance in one of the other two sets of signifiers or interests. The goal of the argumentation will be to restate the relations among the signifiers or interests so as to prevent contrary discourses, in which the subordinated interests would become prominent, from generating significance and force. This is done mainly negatively, by discrediting the potential for dominance in the other two and deforming them toward the dominant.

Internally, a theological discourse serves to prevent the possible or anticipated actualization of the potential for dominance in one of its two subordinated, deformed, or discredited languages. When that discourse encounters a theology dominated by one of those languages it is already prepared to engage it oppositionally and to intensify both its subordination of that language and its differences from and opposition to the theology that has that subordinated language in a position of dominance. The polemical relations among theological discourses with differing dominants will be intense because the dominant in each is supported not by direct argumentation so much as by arguing against the potential for dominance in the subordinant interests. One theological discourse will be very threatening to another whose dominant differs, both because the one has as its dominant what is subservient in the other and because the one makes subservient what is dominant in the other. So, a spokesperson for one kind of discourse, say of the "X" kind, will see in contrary discourses the denial of the dominance of "x" matters and a denial of the subservience of one of its other sets of interests. Since the argumentation of theology has to do primarily with these relations of dominance and subservience, theological discourses arguing differing relations among their interests are threatening to one another in the extreme. Theological discourses argue, then, not only against the potential for dominance in their own subjected languages or interests but also against differently arranged discourses. And, since the dominant or starting point of a theological discourse is affirmed and defended at the expense and in defiance of the potentials for those roles in the other interests, theological polemics are likely to be heated and nonnegotiable. For this reason it is a mistake to dismiss or even underestimate the *theological* component in interinstitutional tensions, those of heresy trials, religious wars, and the like, in favor of their social and political components.

Polemic among theological discourses becomes virulent, therefore, because differences between them of the kind I have been attempting to clarify arise from the aims and dynamics of theological argumentation itself. The differences between theological discourses are such that they potentially and implicitly attack the dynamics or relations in one another. It is not possible for me to be persuaded by an "X" discourse without at the same time also recognizing that discourses of the "Y" and "Z" kind are distorted in their claims and hostile to my basic belief. Each kind of discourse discredits the others, and the threat of one discourse to the basic belief of another fuels the suggestion that the other system is irremediably wrong in some way.

Since differing theological discourses inevitably attack the sources of significance and power of one another and are attacked by them, predictable and virulent conflict is bound to occur. It may even be possible to say that because an opposing theological discourse has as its starting point an interest that its spokesperson believes to be primary, not grounded, that is, on something else, the resistance of that discourse to persuasion by a differing discourse may easily be taken as a certain recalcitrance, religious insensitivity, or perversion in the spokesperson or the sponsoring institution of that discourse. This accounts at least in part, it seems to me, for the frequent ad hominem aspects of theological polemic, the perpetuation of deep animosities among Christian institutions, and the violent consequences to which theological differences in the past have led, including wars and executions. To put it as strongly as possible, one does not understand theology unless one understands why violent relations among Christians are theologically produced and why social, political, and economic factors readily accompany and complicate theological disputes.

III

Now that the shape and dynamics of theological argumentation have been clarified in this quite abstract way, it may be possible to describe the three kinds of theological discourses more fully, to put some flesh on the bones, so to speak. I will use names and even give textual designations to the three groups rather than the highly generalized "X," "Y," and "Z." This is preliminary to offering an alternative way of reading theological discourses, of postulating that such discourses not only fall into three groups but that it is necessary to recognize the discursive field of theology if the meaning and dynamics of its argumentation are to be understood.

Theological discourses of the "X" type are dominated, as I have shown, by signifiers concerning that which humans not only do not but cannot understand or control and what the human world does not and cannot contain. They begin with and define the primacy of matters designated by such terms as the "transcendent" or "supernatural." When they speak of God it is to emphasize God's freedom, grace, initiative, power, primacy, and inscrutability. A basic belief for such discourse, for example, is that language about God cannot begin to be adequate or accurate if that language is not primary and determining. Such a discourse is likely to argue the potential or actual contradiction in making language about God subordinate or derivative. The effect of such a discourse is to normalize, one could say, what is unusual, and to place what we generally take to be normal, that is, the human world, into question.

Discourses of this type discredit the claims to dominance that reside in "y" matters by insisting on the impossibility of containing God in particular forms and occasions. "Y" interests in "X" discourses are described as potentially limiting to God's freedom, domesticating God and subjecting God to finite limits, and as leading to idolatry. Discourses of the "X" kind tend to construe the presence of God in forms and occasions that are elusive, to take them, for example, as witnesses to, signs of, or even veils covering that which no form or occasion can contain.

Discourses of this kind undercut the claims for dominance in "z" matters by emphasizing the derivative, dependent, and unreliable status of the human world. They warn against the dangers of anthropocentrism and the divinizing of human nature. The intention of this discourse is to affirm the primacy of what alone deserves it, and that is God. Indeed, the sign of human evil is primarily the desire not to give recognition to God's primacy but to give it instead to some entity or to oneself or one's group.

When confronted with discourses of the other two kinds, theological discourses of the "X" type are provoked by the subjected and deformed positions their own dominant holds in these others. It will seem impious, even blasphemous, that the primacy of the divine should be, as it appears to be in other discourses, modified, slighted, or subordinated to other interests.

Theological discourses of this kind might most appropriately be called "prophetic." This name is free from the vagueness and pejorative connotations of "mystical," and while the interests I have been describing are not adequate to exhaust the burden of the prophetic material in the Bible, the orientation of the biblical prophets is often similar to what I have been suggesting with this first type of discourse. The prophets certainly shared a strong sense of divine power, primacy, and prerogative. Some often were uneasy about specifying the location or residence of Yahweh in any one place or in any one event. Amos, Micah, and Jeremiah, for example, attacked the cultic life of the people and its assumption that Yahweh's presence had that kind of predictability to it. And they responded to the human world by minimizing its potentials and maximizing its unreliability. The cultural accomplishment of urban life and sophisticated political alignments often failed to impress the prophets very much at all, and they seem endlessly resourceful in laying out the evils of human affairs in the past, present, and future. The prophets, in their emphases on "x" matters and their modification, even deformation, of "y" and "z," offer a ready resource for theological discourses of this type. And it is not surprising that theological discourses that I am going to call "prophetic" draw heavily on the prophetic texts of the Old Testament and on the "prophetic" orientation or quality of St. Paul's writings in the New.

Theological discourses of the "Y" type take as their starting point the form or occasion in or by which "x" matters are made available to human beings. The principal focus of interest is on entities or events in which, let us say, the divine and the human, the supernatural and the mundane, confront one another or are joined. Discourses of this kind have as their point of departure the belief that any discussion of God and of human life should take as its basis that occasion, point, or form in which the two contraries touch or unite. Indeed, this event or entity is taken as itself of great interest and importance because it fascinatingly reveals the compatibility/incompatibility of the two in some proportion to one another. The form of divine presence, whether that is here and now, in the past and in a distant place, or in the future in some place yet to be disclosed, is important not only because it determines what can be said about "x" and "z" matters, about God, say, and about humans and their world, but also because it is mysterious, bringing, as it does, contraries and incompatibles into a relationship of some kind. It goes without saying, for such discourses, that this point of contact is where theology must begin and to which it must constantly return, because what we can and should learn about God concerns God's relation to our world and what we should know about human life is how it appears in its relation to God. It becomes perfectly obvious for such discourses that talk concerning God and human life should be dominated by "y" interests, subjected to and deformed toward them.

Discourses of this type attack the claims for dominance embedded in "x" matters within them by insisting, for example, that talk about God, other than in reference to particular forms or occasions of God's presence in our world, becomes idle speculation, a defiance of religious authority, and arrogance. It will regularly warn against the excesses of mysticism and the loss of Christian unity that arise when people fail to subject their discussions of God to the terms made available in the particular form or occasion.

Discourses of this type undercut the claims for dominance in "z" matters within them by insisting that human nature and affairs come to clarity and definition in, or in relation to, the form or occasion that divine presence takes in the human world. The form or occasion brings to light what is most important in or to human life. Rather than understanding the nature of this form or occasion by gathering information generally available about human nature and events, the form or occasion gives insight by which the human world can, more generally, be understood.

When discourses of the "Y" type encounter prophetic discourses in which "y" interests have been subjected and deformed, the response is likely to be strong. For the mystery and authority of the form or event of presence or relation is being compromised. Pride will seem to have dictated the decision to begin not with the form or occasion of divine presence, with its limitations, but with God, as though God were generally or directly available. It will be easy for "Y" discourses to point out that what was good enough for God—presence in some particular form—is not good enough for prophetic discourses. They want to talk of God more directly or fully and not as limited by and available in particular forms and occasions.

When discourses of the "Y" type encounter those in which "z" interests dominate, it will appear that the distinctiveness and mystery of the form or occasion of divine presence has been ignored in favor of a more general interest in the human world. This subjecting of the particularity of sacred events or places in "Z" discourses to more general interests in human needs and potentials will appear to be secularist, a loss of the sacred and its incorporation within and dilution by the general structures and dynamics of human experience.

While the polemical position of "Y" discourses will be taken principally in response to discourses of the other two kinds, another cause for conflict is particularly apparent within this group of discourses, namely, the differences that arise when one rather than some other form or occasion in the human world is identified as making the divine available to human beings. One must be careful here because some differences of this kind may be caused by "x" or "z" considerations. So, for example, a "Y" discourse that emphasizes the Church as the locus of divine presence in the world may be engaged in a polemic against a discourse that would designate not the Church but the person and work of Jesus Christ or Scripture as that form. But this may not finally be an argument between two "Y" discourses over different forms. For example, it may be that "x" interests are determining the emphasis on Jesus Christ because that form or event is more distant and elusive than the Church or Scripture are likely to be. Or an emphasis on Jesus may be determined by "z" interests, because of basic beliefs concerning human potentials and needs that the life and ministry of Jesus speak to or make available. However, there *can* be equal insistence on "y" interests among discourses of this kind with differences arising among them as to what ought to be taken as the exclusive or principal form or occasion of divine presence in or to the human world. Therefore, a discourse that arises from the affirmation that Scripture is the locus of divine presence in our world can be no less a discourse of the "Y" type than one that affirms that the form of this presence and availability is the offices of the Church. This means, for example, that a Protestant for whom Scripture is the very word of God, available to every faithful reader, is as much engaged in a "Y" discourse as a Catholic theologian for whom the Church is the continuation of the Incarnation and that the two differ as to what they take the form or occasion of divine availability to be.

In selecting a name to give discourses of this kind, "priestly," although more easily related to some rather than to other kinds of "y" interests, seems the most appropriate. Priestly discourses, then, have as their starting point and dominant interest the form or occasion of divine presence in the human world, and they have as their principal intention to employ the nature and importance of this dominant against the claims for dominance that are latent in the "x" and "z" interests also found in "Y" discourses. At the same time, such discourses absorb the potential for dominance in "x" and "z" interests by subjecting them to and deforming them toward the dominance of "y."

Priestly discourses find their biblical support in the cultic material, in the liturgical life it implies, and in the care given to the observance of sacred times and the keeping of holy objects. This finds its epitome in the temple, the sense of divine presence there, which many of the cultic Psalms celebrate, the meaningful compartmentalization of the building and its courts, and the sense of the holy mountain as the center of life. Due to their highly prophetic and apocalyptic qualities, many texts of the New Testament undercut or qualify "Y" discourses, although the latent capacities for dominance in "y" interests, when found particularly, say, in the Gospel According to Matthew or in the Pastoral Epistles, can be released by discourses predisposed to granting primacy to them. New Testament texts display a rich interplay between the language of presence and the language of absence, especially in reference to Jesus as the form or occasion of relation between divine and human. It may also be said that for early Christians Jerusalem, not only for reasons made clear in the Old Testament but also as the location of the passion and death of Jesus, was a pilgrimage and cultic center, but this situation was altered by the turmoil and destruction preceding and culminating in 70 C.E. Cultic centers and orientations toward forms of interrelation between the divine and human world can be supplemented or displaced by new locations or replaced by other forms and occasions. For example, in the postexilic period, as the Ezra narrative of the reading of the law reveals, texts took on an authority that the second temple was never able fully to recover from them, and this textual presence, continuing in the New Testament and the Church, complicates the sense of the continuity of cultic life and the transference and supersession of the temple cultus to and by the structure of Christian offices and liturgy.

Theological discourses of the "Z" type are oriented first of all to the needs and potentials of the human world, to the nature of the human ethos and of the surrounding cosmos. They address primarily human need and potential, both individual and corporate. It seems obvious to these discourses that when confronted by a multitude of human problems, resources, and needs the theologian is obligated to assess and respond to them. It also seems obvious that theology is a human activity and is always grounded in human concerns. Discourses of this kind are not limited to negative aspects of human experience; they also can reveal an interest in the positive potentials in human life and in our world, in the capacities of mind and language, in the mysteries of human interaction, in the variety and complexity of cultural contexts and contacts between them, and in the dynamics and order of natural things. In order for discourses of this kind to be theological, they must, of course, include interests of the "x" type, but they more often arrive at, than begin with, discussions of God. In this way the claims for dominance potentially contained in "x" interests are subverted. Working from the problematics or grandeur of life and the world, discussions of "x" interests become matters to which meditation on life and experience, for example, leads. Or God is the answer to questions and problems that arise from experience or from reflection on it. Or God accounts for the way in which there can be relations of rapport and understanding among people or between people and the natural context of their lives.

Discourses of the "Z" type, when they turn to the question of the form of divine presence in the world, tend to minimize the importance of specific occasions and forms and to emphasize the more general: human experience, moments of rapport between people, the hidden but powerful layers of meaning that seem to reside in personal and cultural life, or the structure and dynamics of the cosmic context of human life. The forms or occasions of divine presence in the world are more general, and such forms and occasions are continuous with the surrounding world and testify to or epitomize what is more generally true of the natural or human world. In this way the peculiar claims for dominance made by particular forms and occasions are discredited; they become examples or concentrations, at most, of what is more generally true about or revelatory of divine power and purpose.

When discourses of this type encounter prophetic discourses they attack them for the subordinate position "z" interests hold in them. To subject "z" interests to an overriding concern about God, for example, strikes the "Z" spokesperson as irresponsible and irrelevant to the larger and pressing issues of daily experience and the context of our lives. The particular problems and potentials of life become blurred or ignored in any primarily transcendent orientation, and when interest is taken in the human world by "X" discourses, "Z" spokespersons will view that interest as arbitrary, sporadic, unsystematic, and even anti-intellectual and irrational.

When "Z" discourses encounter a priestly discourse in which human needs and potentials are subjected to considerations of particular forms and occasions of divine presence in the world, charges of "priestcraft" will likely arise. Here, the charge will be made, some particular form or occasion is distinguished from and imposed on the general presence and availability of God in human life and our world so that those in charge of this form or occasion can elevate themselves with it and control or even manipulate other people. A narrowing and fracturing of life results, it will be said, from the subjection of human thought and experience to such specific forms and occasions. Away with this particularism and obscurantism! Let the fullness and vastness of God, revealed in the little and daily things of life as well as in the august and splendid dimensions of our world and experience, be released!

The most appropriate name for discourses of this kind would be, I think, "sapiential." It can be argued that the kind of orientation and interest I have been describing is not unlike that of the biblical wisdom literature. Here one finds a primary emphasis on human experience, relationships, and the structure, variety, and vastness of the created order of things. Proverbs and Ecclesiastes, for example, derive their authority not from some insight into what God is like or from some specific form or occasion of God's presence in the world, a sacred object or book, for example, but from experience. And when God, in the book of Job, talks to Job from the whirlwind, God does not refer to specific instances and forms of presence in the world. Rather than to specific forms and occasions of presence, the periodic, sacred festivals or the holy things and places, God calls Job's attention to the natural world, its animals, the rain and snow, and the variety and vastness of the creation. The form of Yahweh's presence is not particular but cosmic.

While the major wisdom texts are found in the Old Testament, there are sapiential strands in the New Testament as well. Jesus is presented, especially in the Gospel According to Matthew, as a teacher of wisdom as well as a lawgiver. In the Sermon on the Mount he makes a number of moves typical of a teacher of wisdom—appeals to natural life, for example, to birds and flowers—and he mentions Solomon, the traditional patron of Israel's wisdom, who himself, as told in I Kings, dealt heavily in proverbs and observations of nature. In addition, there is a sapiential quality to the Epistle of James, and apocalyptic literature, especially Revelation, has wisdom interests in it—inclusiveness, the cosmic sense, and the emphasis on experience and history.

The role of wisdom in the Old Testament emerges in its relation not only to Solomon but to other kings as well. In fact, it may not be too much to say that the theology of the kings was sapiential. Needing to cope with daily problems, needs, potentials, and possibilities and with people beyond the borders of Israel's geographical and cultic boundaries, wisdom interests would be most pertinent.

"Prophetic," "priestly," and "sapiential" discourses, to name the three kinds that arise from the dynamics of theological interests that I described, are inevitable not only because of the potential in each kind of interest to dominate the others and to attack their potential for dominance, then, but also because the textual resources for Christian theology contain discourses of all three kinds. When one speaks of biblical theology, one must speak in the plural. These differing biblical theologies find their spokespersons in the history of Christianity, although theological conflicts within that history may not always be caused by the differing theologies of biblical texts. The cause may also lie in this, that theological discourses derive their structure and dynamic at the expense of the latent claims to dominance in their subordinated interests and at the expense of one another. A theological discourse derives its power and meaning primarily from the subjugation and deformation of those languages that are not dominant in it but that are dominant in other, differing discourses.

Opposition among theological discourses, therefore, can be traced to the dynamics that propel and perpetuate them, and, except under institutional conditions that may allow for the exclusion by one of them of the other two, all three will always arise and will be in conflict, often virulent, with one another. The situation of hegemony should not be taken, however, as anomalous or extraordinary. Indeed, so convinced of its legitimacy and so threatened by other systems can the spokesperson of a theological discourse be that he or she may even justify the use not only of polemic to attack or suppress discourses of the other types but also of whatever other sources of power—social, political, and financial—can be mustered in order to discredit or repress them. Indeed it is to be expected that theological differences and conflicts will be clarified and prosecuted by such other sources of power. If an institutional situation were provided for spokespersons of all three kinds, conflicts would be avoided among them only if their basic beliefs deferred to some other discourse, such as the university's discourse about disinterestedness and free speech, or the call for a united response to non-Christian or nonreligious discourses that imply or claim that Christianity or religion are not live options or important matters of study. When this occurs, when basic beliefs defer to other considerations and interests, theology ends and discourse becomes descriptive or interpretive of religion, Christianity, or Christian theology.

IV

These three kinds of theological discourses have rich and complex traditions as well as long histories of polemical relations among them. There is no need to attempt telling this story, even if the ability to tell it were in hand. But it is relevant to this study to indicate something of this history if for no other reason than to show that the present situation in Christian theology is not unique.

Medieval Christianity, although complex and inclusive in many respects, should be described as primarily "priestly." The obvious, that which goes without saying, was the grand form of divine presence identified with the Church, its offices, dogma, disciplines, and sacraments. Basic to medieval Christianity was a strong sense of the presence of God in the world in specific locations, of sacred things and places to which reverence was shown and pilgrimage made. There was a highly institutionalized articulation of "y" interests.

The Reformation, with its many important precursors, came about when institutional conditions were no longer available to prevent the potentials for domination in "x" interests from arising. The theological discourses of the Reformation, especially Luther's and Calvin's, are "prophetic"; that is, they attack the claims for dominance of "y" interests with charges of their domestication, even manipulation, of the divine, and charges of idolatry. The primacy is given to God, to divine initiative, freedom, and grace. Correspondingly, "y" factors are modified. There is less emphasis on "presence." And the favorite biblical texts are prophetic, particularly the Epistles of Paul.

At the same time, sapiential discourses also came to the fore. Erasmus was as important for them as Luther and Calvin were for prophetic. The contrary positions of Luther and Erasmus on free will and other human potentials, over against the power and initiatives of God, offer a clear example of two discourses with differing dominants and subordinates. With the seventeenth century, sapiential discourses, stabilized by available institutional conditions, took on power and established domains of activity free from the challenges not so much of "prophetic" as of "priestly" discourses. The most important institution for the empowerment of sapiential interests is the university, but one can say that the modern period, with its scientific, cultural, and political expansions, is intertwined with, perhaps even enfolded by, sapiential discourses.

The theological situation, therefore, cannot be described in only ecclesiastical terms. True, one could say that theological discourses sponsored by Roman Catholic interests will very likely be "priestly" in nature. To hear "prophetic" discourses one should attend a Lutheran or Presbyterian seminary. And to witness a sapiential discourse one should go to a "liberal" branch of a "mainline" denomination or to a Unitarian fellowship. Theological differences have been institutionalized. But it is not so simple. Mainline Protestant denominations may often be found to be either "sapiential" in their discourses or, in their more "conservative" forms, "priestly," rather than "prophetic." That is, there may be a kind of identification of the presence and authority of God with the pages and printed words of Scripture or with the person of the preacher that would rival the most intense language of a Roman Catholic who insists on the literal identification of the body and blood of Christ with the elements of the Sacrament. Or, one can find Roman Catholic theologians who seem to sound like Luther and Calvin as well as others who are "sapiential" in their interests in human culture and/or the natural world.

An interesting complication in the conflictual relations of these three kinds of discourses to one another today arises from the place of the sapiential. That place is by no means limited to the influence of discourses of this kind in "liberal" denominations or communities. It is not even possible to limit their importance to their role in and formative influence over education in general and the modern university in particular, although that is by no means a small matter. One could say that modern culture in its many manifestations carries theological interests that are sponsored and justified sapientially. It is a mistake, I think, to take expressions of moral, spiritual, and even theological interest pervasive, for example, in American cultural history as diluted and secularized versions of originally "prophetic" or "priestly" interests. Paine and Emerson, for example, are not "prophetic" theologians who have become secular. They are full-fledged sapiential spokespersons, discrediting the claim to dominance in "y" interests by denouncing "priestcraft," quoting the wisdom literature freely, and pointing to creation itself, open to human examination and wonder, as the very "word" of God. The theological discourse of extra-ecclesiastical American culture is, I believe, primarily sapiential, and one finds that out not only when theologians with university appointments begin to speak but also when artists write or editorialists call us back to our spiritual or moral roots.

"Sapiential" discourses may have a cultural position today, then, that "priestly" discourses had for medieval life. They possess a kind of legitimacy and power that tends to marginalize the others. The separation of church and state, of religion and politics, of faith and culture, can also be interpreted, it seems to me, theologically, that is, as the normalization and the cultural institutionalization of sapiential discourses and the particularization and privitization of the other two types.

Because of this, I shall, in my readings of some theologies as "sapiential" in Part II, depart somewhat from the pattern of the preceding two chapters in order to sketch more fully how sapiential interests and priorities affect how Americans think about religion and theology. In the first chapter I shall deal with more specific texts of theological discourses of the first type, while in the second chapter I shall begin to describe a more general situation. But in the third chapter of Part II it is the general situation that forms the focus, and I shall mention individual texts as symptoms or manifestations of it.

It is hoped that by reading and placing theologies as I do, the discursive situation created by theologies will be clarified. It is hoped, too, that the examples will clarify how the dominant interest is valorized at the expense of alternative interests. I want to point out how each discourse discredits the potential of competing interests to be taken as dominants or starting points. I hope that I succeed in revealing how each of the three kinds advocates its dominant language primarily by discrediting the potential for dominance in the other two.

PART II

Theological Discourses

Examples

4

PROPHETIC DISCOURSES

THEOLOGICAL DISCOURSES are of the prophetic type when they contain as their hidden premise the belief that the starting point and dominant are "x" matters, that is, signifiers that have the effect of discounting "z" and "y" in order to argue indirectly for the primacy in power, meaning, worth, or being of what lies beyond human understanding and control. They are discourses that take as primary the responsibility to do justice to the language of transcendence, the supernatural, the divine, the eternal, etc. These discourses assume that one should not compromise such matters either by locating them in the particular forms or occasions by which the divine is accessible to human approach or by engaging them through observations or analyses of this-worldly or human entities and events. Such starting points would restrict the transcendent or divine to the limits either of what can be predictable or of the humanly known and understood. These discourses begin with the divine and construe the human world and the forms and occasions of divine availability in subordinate relations to it.

This does not mean, of course, that such discourses discount "y" and "z" matters altogether. Were they to do that they would not be theological, since theological argumentation concerns the relations of all three interests to one another. Theological discourses of this kind are bound to include questions both of specific forms and occasions of divine availability in the world and of the moral and spiritual needs and potentials of human beings. But "y" and "z" matters will be subjected to and deformed toward, will, in fact, be put into the service of, enhancing "x" interests, because it is largely by discrediting the potential for dominance in the other sets of signifiers or interests that theological discourses of this type generate their power and meaning. Given these considerations it can quite easily be seen that a major constructive problem for such discourses is to establish how it is possible to talk at all about what cannot be understood and controlled, about what is contrary, if not contradictory, to our own world, especially when such discourses are at the same time in the business of undercutting and repressing the potential claims for dominance in "y" and "z" matters. How is it possible, for example, to talk about God when the form or occasion of divine presence and the reliability of the human enterprise are being undercut or rendered as elusive and questionable? The principal answer to this question lies in the rhetorical force of the starting point. Rather than argue to that point, the privilege of the starting point is, as in all three kinds of discourses, believed. Not it itself but its primacy constitutes the basic hidden premise. To put it yet another way: In discourses of this type a common move is not from the certainty of language that deals with things human to the uncertainty of language that deals with things divine but, rather, a claim for certainty in the primacy of language concerning things divine that throws "y" and "z" language into positions of dependence and uncertainty.

As can be expected, discourses of this type will, from among the theological topics, be interested in theology, talk about God, and eschatology, talk about the future or the end of it all. The double use of "theology" here is a bit of a nuisance, due to its general and specific functions. Generally, it includes all the topics; specifically, it includes matters concerning God. It is *theo*logic. Why this topic would be a starting point and the principal interest for such discourses should be clear. Why eschatology should also take a central position may be less clear. It does so because the future can easily be taken as a temporal alternative to the more spatial notions of the "transcendent," "supernatural," or "otherworldly." The future we cannot know or control. The conclusion of time, the last things, the ultimate destiny of all: these especially are matters that can easily allow discourses of the prophetic type to generate their power and meaning. This is not to say that discourses of the two other types ignore these topics. But they will be subjected to matters that dominate and give those discourses their distinctive shapes. So, for example, eschatological matters in priestly discourses may emerge from interests in the future of the church or in sapiential discourses from an analysis of human history, while theological matters, in the narrow sense, are extrapolated by "Y" and "Z" discourses from particular forms of divine presence in our world or from human nature, experience, or the cosmos that contains us. In other words, talk about God and eschatology are not limited to prophetic discourses, even though these topics are most likely to be, explicitly or not, central to them.

Since my purpose is neither to catalog all theologians of this type nor to give exhaustive expositions of particular theologians, I have had to select texts and present a partial reading of each theologian's work. The texts chosen as examples of all three kinds of discourses are by theologians of remarkable range and erudition, and it is hoped that the kind of singlemindedness with which they are here read will not appear to caricature their achievements or in other ways to minimize their stature. I hope that it will appear reasonable, then, to contend that the theology of Karl Barth and the eschatology of Jürgen Moltmann are discourses of the prophetic type.

I

Although Barth is often read as "Christocentric," even as a "Christomonist," I take his theology, his understanding of God, to be primary in his work. And this theological starting point, while most fully operative in his early writings, is not repudiated in the *Church Dogmatics,* even though some of the earlier language, such as that emphasizing the distinctions and distance between God and humanity, is reoriented. For the Christological emphasis of Barth, the language of nearness, of God's being bound to humanity, of proximity and of being for humans, is a language that is radically theological because the significance of such language rests on divine prerogative and decision and indicates a possibility that is solely divine. The language of proximity, for Barth, the language of being for and with others rather than being for and with one's self or group, is not a human language; it is not even human language about God. It is God's word, the language of divine grace that has the inescapable name of Jesus Christ. Despite modifications and complications, despite, even more, the suggestions of a Christocentrism, this starting point in the divine initiative, this theological orientation, is never lost. The "humanity" of God is not a human possibility, is not language about humanity.

It is this dominant in his work that allows it to have so much in common with the Reformers, especially Luther and Calvin, and their emphasis on the righteousness of God, on the divine initiatives of election and grace, and on the obligation of the Christian to give God recognition or, as the Heidelberg Catechism and Barth's commentary on it suggest, gratitude.[1] But Barth's theological emphasis takes an important turn from the Reformers and the prophetic discourses their work sponsored. The *Coram Deo* of Luther or the doctrine of Predestination in Calvin, while perhaps in their original forms not so tainted, later became associated with power as intimidation and coercion, forms of power that, for Barth, have as their models human power and privilege and their exercise. In a word, Protestant theology of this kind, while consistent with Barth in its principal orientation to divine initiative and grace, becomes less "prophetic" than his theology when it construes the power of God on models of power that are human. God begins to look and act like a magnified earthly sovereign or what we would be like were we God. If we were capable of doing anything we pleased and of knowing everything, we would use that power to intimidate others, control everything, and exalt ourselves at the expense of all.[2]

Barth's move against this kind of construal of the primacy of God is to stress that God is wholly unlike humans in matters of privilege and primacy. God is not an epitome of primacy as we understand or desire it. In fact, it is impossible for humans to understand why God does not use power the way they would if they were in God's position. The result of Barth's emphasis on God's grace is that God does not need to use power for self-enhancement, because, unlike humans, God is able to be wholly for others rather than for self. God does not have to be concerned about being strong, or looking important, or being number one. This not needing to be self-regarding is something of which humans are not only incapable but cannot understand. If it turns out that a person or group of people is wholly for others rather than for self—and it is not likely that such would occur—it would be the consequence not of human decision or power but of God's. When such an event occurs it is God working through people. The deity of God is to be found exactly here: God's not needing to secure, protect, or exercise primacy and, instead, being together with people, being with and for others. The deity of God resides in God's not being diminished by not being first of all interested in God's primacy.[3]

This emphasis on God's proximity to humans, God's being for others rather than for self, does not sacrifice God's aseity. It is not that God *depends* on others and being with them in order to be God. God's deity rests precisely in being fully for others, but God is for humans not out of necessity but out of freedom. God's freedom is not, as it is for humans, independence and a desire to maintain self-sufficiency. God's freedom is quite contrary to that; it takes the form of commitment to humans. In fact, we cannot derive understandings of what God's aseity, freedom, and love are from our own notions of these things. Rather, we have to relearn what they are from God's unique use of power and primacy.[4]

Having made this move, Barth can go to great lengths to describe the closeness of God to human beings. Since the deity of God, the way God differs from us, is not diminished but increased and clarified by God's proximity to humans, it is possible for Barth even to speak of God's vulnerability to human hurtfulness and of God's ability to be affected by what humans do. It is this theology that allows Barth to give such emphasis to Christology, and his Christology reinforces the language of divine primacy. His theology, in other words, allows Barth to make proximity, even identification, the principal measure of divine *difference*.[5]

It is not difficult to trace in Barth's theology how discourse of this kind discredits the claims to dominance in "z" matters. His theology is calculated to counter human understandings of what God is like or of what the consequences of relation to God will be for human beings. Using his considerable historical and cultural learning and sophistication, Barth presents the principal concern of theology since the Renaissance to have been for human beings, their world, and its potentials. The human in the modern world became the measure of all things. This stream of interest comes to fullest form in the nineteenth century, and it is abruptly challenged with the events leading to and following August, 1914.[6]

Barth is, despite the uncompromising rigor of his polemic against theologians who take human experience and culture as starting points in their theologies, appreciative of them. Indeed, he owed much of his formidable learning to them. But more than that, he acknowledges how important it was for someone like Schleiermacher to attempt, in 1799, to address the cultured despisers of Christianity. The eighteenth and nineteenth centuries were culturally rich. Compared to art, science, philosophy, commerce, and other human interests, religion was not at the center but at the periphery. And the theologians who tried to address the Christian message to such a world had themselves to be immensely sophisticated and ingenious. By taking their contemporaries so seriously, they were dealing with what was most impressive and challenging in their own culture.[7] But while he admires them, Barth sharply differs from their method of beginning theological discourse with matters granted by the cultural environment. Particularly, they placed too much reliance on the nature of religious experience, and this grounded talk about God on a base of human interests in and assumptions about God. Despite the sincerity of their motives and the skills of their arguments, these apologists for Christianity generated rather than questioned an anthropocentrism disclosed in the thought of Feuerbach, who pointed out that talk about God was actually talk about human nature in an exaggerated form. When subordinated to "z" language, theology leads to the support of social, national, and even economic interests, and the critical edge of theology and its leverage on human attitudes are lost.[8] Punctuating Barth's own theology is the crucial point that God is the contrary if not the contradictory of what we want God to be like or would be like if we were God. There is no continuity or point of connection between humanity and God and, therefore, no possibility of moving from the former to the latter.

The force of Barth's objection to theology of this kind was greatly increased, of course, by cultural history, for the First World War did indeed subvert the sense of confidence in a humanly understood and controlled world that marked the nineteenth century and came to fullest expression in such forms as the high priestly scientism of Comte and the forms of colonialism and imperialism that were advanced well into the twentieth century. But it should be pointed out that the force of Barth's theology cannot be traced entirely to these historical or social conditions; it also arises from the challenge to "z" matters that always resides in the ability of "x" to dominate. The First World War, rapid urbanization, and the growing perceptions of the problems of colonialism and imperialism may have given the occasion and impetus to the emergence and great influence of a theology so shaped, but the potential for such a theology and for the sharp conflicts with others it produced was already there.

In Barth's theology "z" matters or anthropological considerations are subordinated to the language of divine initiative. Barth follows Luther in discounting the contribution people may be thought to make to their own redemption or the claims about themselves that the grace of God could be used to warrant. There is no distinction to be made between elected, justified, redeemed, or Christian people on the one hand and unelected, condemned, or non-Christian people on the other. Christian, justified, or elected are never predicates of human life.[9] They always wholly and only refer to divine action. When people testify to the grace and power of God by their words or deeds, they do not, by definition, draw attention to themselves but away from themselves. The ability not to be self-preoccupied and self-referential is an ability possessed only by God, and when it appears in human behavior it does not signal a human achievement but, rather, God's grace.

It becomes a little more difficult to point out the subordination in Barth's theological discourse of "y" matters. Indeed, some who have read this far may all the while have been insisting on Barth's Christocentric emphasis and his attention to Scripture, preaching, sacraments, and the Church. But I think that his theology is calculated to undercut the potential for dominance in these matters as well.

Perhaps the subordination of "y" language may not be so clearly seen or pronounced in Barth's theology as can be the suppression of "z," because what he thinks of as "anthropocentric" theologies are (with the exception of Catholic theological uses of the *analogia entis*), like Barth himself, Protestant. In addition, his attack on theological interests dominated by "z" matters is an attack on interests he himself once held. So, it has all the force and accuracy of a self-criticism. But the results for "y" matters, though perhaps more muted, are also there. Rhetorical power is also generated at the expense of "y" interests.

The principal way in which this is done is by treating the approach or presence of God to human beings temporally rather than spatially, as occasion rather than entity. The "temporal" quality of the presence of God makes it more elusive. Furthermore, this way of construing the presence of God or God's togetherness with humanity carries with it all of the strange, even mysterious qualities of present time. As St. Augustine pointed out in his *Confessions,* present time possesses the characteristic of being both the only real time (past is no longer and future is yet to come) and the only kind of time we cannot grasp. Present time has a "now you see it, now you don't" quality, and the eventful character of the divine presence in the human world, related as it is to present time, partakes of that quality unavoidably.

This is not to say that Barth builds his doctrine of revelation on a philosophy of time. Rather, he has theological reasons for preserving the divine initiative, freedom, and hiddenness in his doctrine of revelation, and the temporal categories he uses provide considerable help in preserving these characteristics of divine revelation because of the elusive and nonextended characteristics of present time.[10]

Another way in which Barth's theology undercuts the potential for dominance in the "y" matters it contains is his stress on the powerless or self-emptying characteristics of the forms of divine presence. In his Christology, for example, Barth stresses the obedience, rejection, and servant-like characteristics of the life of Jesus, and, even more than the life, he emphasizes the death, the Crucifixion. He seems, almost, to use the images of the suffering servant passages from Second Isaiah to interpret the life of Jesus more than the synoptic writers used them. "Despised," "rejected," "servant"—the language of ordinariness, humility, vulnerability, obedience, is heavily used.[11] In this Barth follows St. Paul, who not only stresses the passion and death of Jesus with little regard for his life but also delights in pointing out that God has chosen not what is powerful, impressive, or wise in the world but what is foolish, insignificant, and weak. No ground is granted for boasting about human nature or human culture, and it becomes impossible to predict or grasp the form of divine presence because it is always hidden within weakness, is always elusive.

Such language is also used in Barth's ecclesiology. Barth's earlier work presents an almost contrary relation of the Christian Church to the kingdom or power of God and carries out what Kierkegaard called an attack on Christendom.[12] Too easily the churches allow language about God and grace to become ways of setting Christians apart from and above others. The feeling of being elected, called apart, becomes a matter of pride, and Christianity becomes a form of self-interest. This attack on religion, on Christianity and the Church by Barth and other prophetic theologians is well known. But the *Church Dogmatics* develops a more positive ecclesiology, although the negative estimation of the presumptions to which the Church is prone shadow the discussion.

One of Barth's interests in developing his ecclesiology is a negative one—his suspicion of private, individual Christianity. His emphasis is as nonindividualist as it is noninstitutional. The Church is *community*. It is a context to which people are called and in which they can most fully actualize the chief role of their humanity, which is to be acknowledgers of God's gift of his togetherness. This message and recognition allow them also, although imperfectly and noncontinuously, to be together with one another.[13] The principal expression of this form is gratitude. In other words, the Church is a community of God's Word if, in response to that Word, the members of that community do an uncharacteristic thing: think of themselves, their interests, and their well-being as not of first importance. Such people may become doers as well as hearers of the Word, acting in the world differently from the way others act, standing up when others sit, speaking when others are silent, showing regard for what in life is generally neglected.[14] But this is not because Christians have become different from others or possess something others do not. His doctrine of justification is more Lutheran than Calvinistic. Justification is imputed rather than imparted. The language is *simul peccator et justus.* No one who accepts the justification of God made available in the death and resurrection of Christ loses his or her role as a rebel against God. To hear the "yes" always means hearing the "no," not also but first.[15]

II

It is largely due to Jürgen Moltmann's *Theology of Hope* that the topics of eschatology, matters, that is, concerning the end of time, have been brought into the center of theological discussions from the peripheral and at times sectarian locations they have often held or to which they have been assigned. Moltmann, among other things, succeeded with this text to make the case that eschatological interests are not the last things to be considered but the first and should affect theology from root to branch. For this text, eschatology is the beginning point for theological discourse, and all other theological interests are subordinated to it.[16]

Moltmann's eschatology, dealing as it does with the future, concerns the transcendent—what we do not know and cannot control. But eschatology is not merely speculation concerning the future; it necessarily includes an orientation toward the future, namely one of expectation and hope. Furthermore, Moltmann's starting point gains status because the early Church and the New Testament can easily be described as affected by a future orientation, and the transcendent for biblical texts is as much, if not more, temporal and oriented to the future as spatial and oriented to "above" (21). Moltmann argues that one's attitude toward the future, one's expectations, affect experience and color present time. So, the future can be thought of as having a power or authority over the present (18). Finally, Moltmann's orientation to temporality, the future, and the disposition of hope gains force from his argument in that it produces, rather than a passive helplessness in relation to the future, a sense of participation in a dynamic process. While not having the kind of optimism in the future that marked, for example, the Social Gospel movement in America, Moltmann's theology of hope never rests satisfied with present social and cultural forms but looks beyond them to more abundant life (35).

Moltmann, while indebted to Barth, is critical of the consequences that the use of present time has for Barth's theology. An emphasis on present rather than on future time tends to turn the presence of God into isolated events that themselves have no real development. An implicit Platonism, given such a construction, is hard to avoid. Indeed, by emphasizing present time, God's time as eternal present is dissociated from human time as passage from past to future (50–58).

While Moltmann wants to stress the temporality of God's revelation, he does not want to slip into what I have called sapiential modes of thought; he does not define eschatology, for example, in terms of objective human possibilities, as in Kant's ethics (58–69). The future is genuinely transcendent, for Moltmann, and that transcendence is the starting point of his argument. The sign of this transcendence is "promise." Revelation is always promise, a moment in the past or present that forces attention on the future, a future, furthermore, that is not identical with the future humans desire, anticipate, or are able to effect. Revelation has a content, but it needs always to be fulfilled to be complete. The deity of God becomes, for Moltmann, not so much, as with Barth, God's ability not to be self-concerned and to be instead completely for humans but, rather, God's ability to make promises that, even when contradicting the present and discontinuous with human abilities, can and will be kept, promises that, consequently, can alter the present, and human orientation to it, because these promises of God are of a sort that only God can keep them. History, while itself neither the revelation of God nor the medium by which the promises of God are kept, becomes the locus of revelation because it is in and through history that God's deity, God's making of promises that God will keep, is manifest. Rather than in isolated events or moments of present time, God is known in and through the relation events have to one another. But what humans know of God by such means is a knowledge that is always incomplete, always still promise that directs attention to the transcendent future (69–94).

Moltmann's interest in, even dependence upon, the biblical prophetic literature is clear. He brings into focus much that is central to it, particularly its orientation to the future. For the prophets, God is known primarily as the one who makes and keeps promises. Israel's history becomes the locus of knowledge of God because the past and the future illuminate one another. For the prophets the fidelity of God does not mean that God can be counted on to do what people expect; God is always transcendent. And, for the prophets, the people, by keeping the law, do not so much, as in priestly orientations, enter a separate, sacred time distinct from the temporality of impure people. Rather, the prophet's temporality is inclusive in its interest in human history and God's relation to it, not only the history of Israel but the history of other nations and of the cosmos as well (95–138).

When turning to the New Testament, Moltmann, like Barth, easily places his argument in a Pauline context. The Resurrection of Christ is decisive. Rather than in the life of Jesus first of all, the key to understanding him can be found in the Resurrection. And the Resurrection is not the culmination of potentials already present but the introduction of something new that changes those potentials (139–48).

The Resurrection, for Moltmann, changes as much as it fulfills the terms of promises made in the past. The Resurrection recasts the promise: from land to world, from progeny to all people, from life to the victory over death. In the light of the Resurrection Abraham can be reinterpreted, although the promise to Abraham also helps to interpret the Resurrection. But the Resurrection is not only fulfillment; it is also promise, also future-oriented. For Paul, the believer is baptized into the death of Jesus and raised to a hope in the Resurrection. The victory over death is still incomplete (148–65).

The Resurrection of Christ is a real event and not something that the disciples only believed to have occurred. But it is not an event in the continuum of human acts and potentials. In this respect it is not historical, if historical events have continuity with one another and lie within the limits of human comprehension. History has become, for modernists, a closed system in which nothing completely new is expected to occur; this view of history is anthropocentric, a construing of events in human image. We are interested in extracting general patterns or laws from history, and the relation of the Resurrection to such a history, consequently, becomes a serious problem. But Christians cannot give up the event of the Resurrection without losing their faith. Nor can they create a category of puzzling or mysterious events of which the Resurrection is one, since this both dilutes the newness, the unexpectedness, of the event and discounts the importance of the Resurrection for human time. What must be done is to take the Resurrection as future-oriented, as an event the nature of which has still to be revealed, but also as an event that, by being a promise of God, can effect changes in our own orientation to history, can even change history itself. That is, the Christian need follow neither the positivist historian, for whom an event is something objectively comprehensible, nor Rudolf Bultmann, for whom the event is principally subjective. Rather than allow an anthropocentrically construed understanding of history to pass judgment on the possibility and nature of the Resurrection, the Christian should let the certainty of promise available in the event of the Resurrection question the enclosedness and adequacy of modern assumptions about history. The "historical" effect of the Resurrection is that time now has been altered for the believer, who can look with hope toward the future because the future, rather than limited to and by human possibilities, is opened by the promise of God. This hope allows believers to work for right relations between people, to allow the power and faithfulness of God to determine what is possible, and to anticipate the Parousia, the future that will illuminate what it was that occurred on Easter (173–203).

It should be clear why and how Moltmann undercuts the potential for dominance in the "z" matters within this discourse. He does so primarily by addressing the understanding of "history" with categories open to the transcendent, especially promise and the future. He points out that the kind of appeal generally made to the "historical" as the norm for what can be taken seriously as possible or actual is curious, given the great uncertainty concerning history that also marks the modern period. Our understanding of history has been in crisis at least since the French Revolution, and attempts to assume that history provides a secure base for validity in scholarship end without assuring anything solid and incontestable. Appeals to history represent attempts to overcome the disorienting effects of history that result from the loss of authority within it, whether through the evaporation of tradition or of belief in divine providence. The putative objectivity that notions such as "cause-effect," "tendency," "forms," and so forth have in theories concerning history conceal their role as purely investigative categories. As a matter of fact, according to Moltmann, there are no adequate philosophies of history, and the question "history of what?" is answered with assumptions concerning history that depend on kinds of realism that are quite untenable, such as, for example, that there is some "human nature," destiny, or spirit that has a history or that is unfolding (230–72).

Eschatology, for Moltmann, then, cannot be built as an extension on or of notions available in the culture concerning time and history. Rather, eschatology undercuts the allegedly self-enclosed, humanly oriented, and normative characteristics of history. The kind of discourse Moltmann represents derives its power not only by appealing to the transcendent or the future as primary but also by discrediting the authority and coherence of human history and of what one generally thinks it authorizes. Moltmann thereby questions not only the history of theological discourses dominated by "z" interests but the notion of human history upon which these discourses seem to depend and which they, in return, reinforce. By arguing that Christian eschatology cannot depend on a modern understanding of history but that, rather, such understandings of history must be challenged by Christian eschatology, Moltmann discredits the potential for dominance that resides in the "z" component of his theology.

The undercutting of potential for dominance in "y" matters can be seen in Moltmann's discussion of the Church. Temporal rather than spatial metaphors are stressed, movement rather than arrival, uncertainty rather than predictability. More than that, he is no less harsh on the Church, its distortions and falsifications, than is Barth.

The Church, according to Moltmann, has unfortunately had its role relegated to it by the culture. Primarily it has become a housing for the nurture of subjectivity. Because society has become a system of needs and of services and commodities designed to meet those needs, everything else is turned over to individual choice and taste. The Church becomes a place where people, interested in that kind of thing, can experience personal encounters by relaxing their social, economic, and political roles and goals. It becomes a subcommunity, a more personal arena than the society at large, which becomes increasingly cold, materialistic, and impersonal. There is thought to be no connection between the two, between the society of public contacts and the personal subcommunity that exists alongside it as a haven. Furthermore, the Church also participates in the culture of goods and services by offering commodities that are not available elsewhere. Its clergy are professionals able to respond to certain expectations and needs (304–24).

In contrast to what the Church largely has become, Moltmann suggests what the Church ought to be. What do "y" interests become when subordinated to the dominant in Moltmann's text? Conditioned by its sacramental life, which looks not so much to the past in memory as to the future in expectation, the Church should be ahead of the world, longing and working for righteousness, life, and freedom. The Church should begin to become what it hopes the world more largely will someday be. The mission of the Church is not to try to make the world into a Church or to draw the world into itself but, rather, to point beyond itself to the future that God has promised. The calling of the Church and of the Christian is to transform the surrounding world by hope in God's promised future (325–38).

Moltmann's ecclesiology is dominated, therefore, by his starting point in the transcendent, in the future as belonging to God and coming toward humans with possibilities that, if taken seriously now, can begin to transform human lives even before the promises, which point toward the future, are fully realized. As vigorously as he attacks the claims of "z" matters by questioning the reliability, endurance, and stability of human history and understandings of it, so Moltmann attacks the claims of "y" matters by questioning any sense of certainty, completion, or arrival in what he calls the "Exodus" Church.

III

The influence of prophetic discourses such as these on contemporary Christian theology is too great to measure and too well known to need elaboration. The point I want to make is that the influence is due not simply to the impressive erudition and forceful style of theologians such as these. The readiness for such theological emphases created by historical, cultural, and social conditions does not wholly account for their impact, either. And their institutional situations do not adequately explain it. Important as all of these factors are, the force and effectiveness of their work must also be attributed to the possibilities for dominance that exist in those matters within theological interests that I have been labeling with the letter "x." The power of these discourses arises from the argument that the three interests, which must be related to one another, should be so related that "x" is the starting point and dominant and that "y" and "z" matters must be subordinated to, and deformed toward, it. The power and influence arise from the potential in the language of "x" to be advanced at the expense of the other two.

The dominance of "x" language is not so much argued as deployed. When one is speaking of God or of eschatology, justice can be done to them only by taking them as starting points. Otherwise they become extensions of human categories, capacities, and desires, merely ways by which, as Barth liked to say, people talk about themselves in a loud voice. Thus transcendence, ultimacy, finality, and eternity are modified or obscured. If there really is a God and if there really is to be a meaningful conclusion to everything, then it is only proper and inevitable to attempt to draw out their implications, because they alone are important; whatever else is important and meaningful derives from them. When they are taken as starting points all else is dislodged from certainty.

The devaluation in such discourses of the possible claims for dominance in "y" and "z" matters can then be argued. The forms of God's presence can never grant predictability to that presence, for that would limit God's freedom and transcendence and produce the arrogance of religion and the sin of idolatry. Such forms too quickly would testify more to the capacity of the human world to contain or sustain them than to the God present or available in them. So also the claims for dominance in "z" matters are undercut either by identifying the locus of God's relations to humanity with the points of greatest human weakness, such as suffering and death, or by exposing the ideologies and self-interests by which current social, political, and economic systems are sustained and the breaks and incoherences of human history. That is, "z" matters are undercut by discrediting anything within them that would serve as a substantial and secure starting point for a theological or eschatological discourse.

In polemic against priestly and sapiential discourses, prophetic discourses will accuse the first of "idolatry" and the second of "anthropocentrism." Priestly and sapiential discourses are attacked as compromising the primacy of "x" matters. Since their starting point is wrong, what they say is always and radically mistaken.

5

PRIESTLY DISCOURSES

THEOLOGICAL DISCOURSES of the second kind have as their hidden premise the belief that "y" language, that is, the form or occasion of divine presence in our world, should be the starting point and the primary focus of theological attention. This belief has, as much as does that concerning "x" signifiers for prophetic discourses, the force of the obvious. If the divine is at some place or time related to or in our world, that place or time of relationship is where theology should begin. This starting point undercuts the potential for dominance in the other elements by pointing out that what can be said about God must derive from God's availability in our world, and what can be said about our world must be derived from that form or occasion as well. Both God and the human world are revealed in and by the unique occasions or forms of their relationship. The nature of the relationship is not derived from "x" or "z" interests; rather, what is said about them must be derived from the meeting or connection of the two.

The form or occasion of divine availability can vary from one priestly discourse to another, and in Christian theology they focus primarily on the person and work of Jesus Christ, on the structure or life of the Church, and on Scripture. Therefore, theological discourses of this kind will tend to begin with or take a strong interest in Christology and ecclesiology. It can be said, as a general point, that priestly discourses stress a language of entities and places when addressing the relation of God to human life rather than the language of events and time. So, the Incarnation in Christology, the Word of God as text, and the Church and sacraments as actualities, places, and objects are stressed, the substantiated rather than the temporal.

In polemical situations, priestly discourses react strongly to the subjugation and deformation of "y" matters in the other two kinds of discourses. They will react by attacking prophetic discourses as "mystical," as not ordered and directed by the form of divine presence in and to our world and its consequences for theological reflection. Concerned about the loss of authority and specificity, priestly discourses, while they may acknowledge that direct interest in the transcendent is possible for a few people and that such exceptions remind the Church that God, while available in a particular form in our world, is not exhausted by that form, will insist that relation to God is first and foremost in terms established by the occasion or form and the mystery of relationship that it contains.

Interest in the needs and potentials of the human world, when they become dominant, as they do in sapiential discourses, strike priestly polemicists as "secular," divorced and independent from the point where those interests are addressed by the specific form or occasion of divine presence. They will point out the danger of deriving an agenda for the Church, for example, from secular interests and values. Priestly discourses will point to the dangers of speaking about the world without beginning with the specific point when or where it meets and is affected, negatively and/or positively, by divine presence. The form or occasion of relation between the two reveals the human world as well as God.

Priestly discourses can find much to support them in Christian scripture and tradition. Israel's life seems, from very early days in the land, to have been determined by specific places where Yahweh's presence could be sought or found and by a calendar that allowed people periodically to approach this presence. With the centralization of the shrines, culminating in the Davidic monarchy and the building of the temple in Jerusalem, this kind of orientation shaped the life, especially the official life, of Israel. After the Exile and the increasing importance of the written law, this emphasis on the temple was attenuated, but it continued. Jerusalem was the locus, the habitation of Yahweh, as many of the Psalms profess, and that belief continues in the time of the second temple.

The early Church was also heavily oriented to Jerusalem. Not only the goal of pilgrimage for the Jews, Jerusalem, as the place where Jesus died and the Resurrection occurred and as the location of the dominant church, was also a goal of Christian pilgrimage.

Although the early Church, under enormous pressure not only because of the destruction of Jerusalem but also because of persecution, was not able immediately to develop the fully cultic life that emerged a few centuries later, it is surprising how, even under adverse conditions, the life of the community was ordered and the continuity with Jewish cultic life preserved, although with radical reinterpretations. The specificity of the place and time of divine presence was identified with the existence and identifiable structure of the churches or church. The hasty developments of this emphasis after the opening decades of the fourth century are too well known to need elaboration here.

Even after the Reformation, with its reliance on prophetic discourses, and the rise of Christian humanism, with such sapiential spokespersons as Erasmus, priestly discourses and the force of their interests continued to be felt until the present day. To find strong, confident, and polemically assertive discourses of this kind entering the forum of general theological debate, one would look naturally to Roman Catholic theologians, although their voices often have been muted, it seems, by the influence of the other kinds of discourses on Catholic interests. Catholic theologians at times seem more eager to modify the dominance of "y" matters with interests of the other two kinds than to emphasize them. This may be because the institution of the Church, its size, authority, and elaborate cultic life, has discourses not only embodied in it but articulated by its ongoing activities, so that Catholic institutions rather than theologians are put into the roles of principal occasions for defining religious and theological identity. It is also true that Roman Catholic theologians, especially those holding posts in universities or who are influenced by ecumenical movements, may be as willing, out of interest in larger discursive contexts, to minimize the distinctive emphases of priestly discourse as to maximize them. Their willingness sets up the possibility of Catholic reemphasis on "y" interests that makes the theological situation within the Church appear to be as conflicted as that between Catholic and other kinds of Christian theologians.

I

The Christology with which I shall begin, however, is not that of a Roman Catholic theologian but of a Protestant. It is a well-known text, and it forms a nice transition from the prophetic discourses I described in the preceding chapter to the present interests. I have in mind D. M. Baillie's *God Was in Christ.*

Baillie sets his Christology in explicit opposition to Karl Barth's. Baillie finds objectionable the repression by Barth of the human and historical in Christology. Barth has, he argues, insufficient interest in the historical Jesus, and Baillie thinks that as far as Barth is concerned the character of Jesus is hidden behind veiling, weakness, suffering, and dying and is consequently unavailable to us. The humanity of Jesus seems to have an only negative relation to the full presence of God in and through him. Barth acknowledges no capacity that the human can be thought to have for the divine, no connecting point. The human does not reveal; it obscures the divine. Baillie finds this attitude to be too skeptical concerning the human and the historical.[1]

For Baillie, a more positive assessment of the human in Christology does not necessarily mean human*ism* or anthropocentrism. While avoiding the excesses of emphasizing the human, one should not fall into the contrary extreme of thinking that the human can be open to the divine only when and where the human is negated (44).

The starting point for priestly discourses is *relationship,* and the principal task Baillie faces is to develop a Christological discourse that brings into one sentence, so to speak, language about God and language about human life without dissolving the one in or by the other. Talk about God, God's actions, and God's presence must be related to talk about human possibilities and actualities without confusing the one with or by the other. In Barth's Christology, according to Baillie, despite all its emphasis on proximity, even identification, a separation or freedom of God from the human is preserved. Baillie argues that in his humanity Jesus makes a contribution to God's entry into our world (48–54).

Baillie confronts the principal task by trying to avoid all of the Christological "heresies" in the tradition, heresies that he thinks err by trying to answer the question of how these two languages can be joined without letting one obscure or distort the other. He does not mean that Jesus was a God, or that he was an intermediate being between God and humans, or that he was half god and half man, for example, a divine mind in a human body, or that he started out being a man and ended up being divine, or that God, by a metamorphosis, changed into a man. He wants to avoid all of these mistaken and distorting explanations (114–18). The mode or form of the relationship of human and divine in the person and work of Jesus is not something that can be understood. It is, rather, a starting point, a basic affirmation from which all else that we say about God and about the human should derive. Because this relationship is the absolute point of vantage from which all else is considered, no *explanations* can be substituted for the mystery of the relationship itself. Any theological attempt to understand the nature of the relation between the divine and the human in the person and work of Jesus would inevitably err by elevating above the Incarnation an explanatory model, giving to something else the primacy that must be reserved for the language of relationship itself.

In order to preserve the Incarnation as an authoritative point, Baillie wants particularly to avoid two kinds of Christological emphases. Both of them he sees in Barth, a kind of Nestorianism, or stress on the distinction of the human and the divine from one another, and a kenotic Christology, one that takes as its locus the lyrical description of Christ in Philippians 2 and stresses the emptying of divine powers in the taking on of the human (94–98). But this does not mean that Baillie is able to describe or explain the Incarnation. The relationship of the divine and the human to one another is, he says, an antinomy, a paradox, and a mystery (106–32). It is only the language of paradox and mystery that keeps Christian theology from being either dualistic or pantheistic.

The principal mode of argumentation that Baillie uses is analogy. What he seems to have in mind as a helpful analogue to the Incarnation is any moment in human life when something truly memorable and admirable has been done by someone and when that person, at the same time, is genuinely surprised by the deed and takes no credit for it. What he uses as analogues to the Incarnation are what can perhaps be called "ecstatic" moments, times when a person is most fully actualized and at the same time not self-conscious. At such times a person can be most free, while also thinking that whatever is good comes from beyond the self. A person can be most like himself or herself when not self-concerned. The Christian language for this, Baillie points out, is "not I but God." A person who says such a thing as a result of such an experience is not negating self but has instead discovered the mystery of self as well as the grace of God (114–18). Such moments of paradox may provide analogues for understanding the Incarnation, but they cannot be substituted for the mystery of the Incarnation itself or used as explanations. That I am most myself when I am least self-conscious, for example, or that a certain unplanned gesture may be more suited to a situation than a planned one—these moments grant surprising accesses to the mystery of human experience. Such experiences point to aspects or dimensions of the human that form a threshold, he seems to argue, across which the divine passes in the Incarnation. While Baillie does not want to use analogue as explanation, as a way to dissolve mystery and paradox, he does seem, by this analogue, to posit a quality or category in and of human experience as an actual point of entry used by the divine into human life.

Baillie's Christology commits him to a human input to the Incarnation. Jesus Christ is the form of God's uniquely authoritative presence in the world because he was a man most fully receptive to God who, in him, fully broke into human life. That having occurred, the divine and the human are joined, and this relationship constitutes that center from which all theological discourses must be derived and no theological discourses can exhaust or explain.

II

The form or occasion in or by which the divine and the human are related can be central to a Christology that is far more historical and political, and less essential and idealist, than Baillie's. I have in mind the Christology of a text by the Brazilian Catholic theologian of liberation, Leonardo Boff—*Jesus Christ Liberator.*

Boff recognizes that a Christology, because it has to do with God's presence in the world, will always have political and social implications. The inevitable question is whether or not this presence reinforces or challenges the present social and political order. Indeed, a Christology for Boff should explicitly promote a sensitivity to the structures of power in the present day and to the question of who benefits from them and at the expense of whom those benefits are maintained. The effect of a Christology should be practical; it should cause the Church always and anew to recognize and identify with those who are injured and oppressed by social, political, economic, and even religious structures.[2] In fact, Christology produces a certain deportment in the world and not merely a set of ideas. Christology calls for imitation, for an extension of the incarnation in and for one's world (63–79 and 279–86).

Boff's first move to articulate this kind of Christology is to affirm the importance of the humanity of Jesus. There are two major interests here. The first is to restore a sense of the humanity *of* Jesus from the excessive interest in the beliefs *about* Jesus that mark the post-Bultmannian theological scene (7ff.). Secondly, Boff is eager to emphasize that in the Gospels a certain kind of man emerges, an intriguing personality, an effective leader, and an innovator.

Boff is able to list surprisingly many characteristics of Jesus. He is a man, for example, of good sense and composure. He is busy but also able to take time with people. He can distinguish the essential from the peripheral, put things into perspective, go to the heart of concrete issues, and force decisions when they are required. His message, though dealing with great and portentous matters, is not esoteric or arbitrary. He relates his message to the obvious and natural aspects of daily life. He is a person observant of life around him, both social and natural, and he does not present the world as worse or better, more simple or more complex, than it is. He is, moreover, capable of a wide range of emotions and feelings—affection for children, mercy and compassion toward people in distress, forgiveness toward the guilty, anger toward the crass and exploitive, grief and disappointment. He is familiar with fatigue, hunger, loneliness, temptation, and discouragement, but he is also constantly vigorous, spontaneous, curious, and attentive to the needs and attitudes of others. An imaginative person, he is able to see people as potentially greater than they are, to see alternatives to present situations, and to anticipate possibilities. He is not afraid to use the personal pronoun "I," and, rather than simple obedience, he stresses the need to understand and size up the world, to recognize signs of the times, and to act in ways appropriate to the situation. He is good in debate—able to unmask insincerity, to get out of a trap, and to turn the tables on his opponent. He is open to help from others, and he has a sense of why things are the way they are, what causes them. His analysis of situations and his response to them are profound and original (80–99).

A crucial move by Boff is to assert that Jesus, while having these many human characteristics, did not have a specific personality. He bases this assertion on the sinlessness of Jesus. To have a personality or an identity structure is to exclude some kinds of people and human interests or possibilities, because all structures exclude. This ability to have or to advocate no personality, to perpetuate no personal agenda, means that he could all the more be the container or the channel of God's presence (190–99).

After describing the human characteristics of Jesus and asserting that Jesus was free from the limits of personality, Boff goes on to assert that it requires the entire course of human history and the entire range of human interests and needs to interpret the humanity of Jesus. Boff treats the history of interpretation, of Christologies, as a display of the many ways in which Christ has been present in and to the world. This process continues today, and we have available to us many ways to recognize that Christ is or can be present now (206–46).

Christology, rather than abstract, relates Christ to actual circumstances and can become a force that changes them. While Christ is with us in society, his presence questions, even subverts, its structures. This means that there can be no end to the process of interpreting the presence of Jesus in our daily world, for the present conditions and our understanding of the challenge he offers to them are constantly changing. There is continuity in Christology, but that continuity is also dynamic, marked by gradual or abrupt change (247–63).

The historical/social situation in our own day is one that calls particularly for an affirmation of the relation of Jesus to the common people and to the poor. Christology today should emphasize the social and economic factors that make for poverty and the consequences of the Incarnation for them. Christology should lead to action, particularly on behalf of those who, because they lack power, cannot act for themselves (264–78).

Although Boff emphasizes the complex life of Jesus and its relevance to a Christology that takes social, political, and economic conditions seriously, he does not minimize the death and Resurrection. The death reveals how unaligned Jesus was with the power structures of his day. He refused to identify himself or the kingdom of God with any particular party or human interest. Most of all his death reveals that it is possible not to depend upon personal and social structures to receive one's identity and that full humanity comes about precisely in that freedom. The Resurrection, God's response to that death, is hidden from us. It is a new creation, but one in which the Church already now participates. The Resurrection carries the message of liberation from all powers that claim finality or threaten to invoke the finality of death (100–17 and 134–37).

By stressing the effects of Christology, we should not lose sight of the main point of the Christology itself. It is this: We should not approach Christology with preconceived notions of what God and human beings are or ought to be like. Boff draws notions about both from the form of their relation, namely, the person and work of Jesus. This form is inexhaustible, for it combines both the fullness of the human and the fullness of the divine. Although not identifiable or to be confused with one another, the two are also apposite to one another. Doctrinal and creedal statements, rather than explain the relation the two have to one another, protect it from distortion. The "person" of Jesus in those formulations is the mysterious way in which the human and divine in him are brought together. The Christ of the Gospels, then, is a single mystery from which we draw conclusions about the mystery of God, of human life, and of their relationship. These conclusions are always inadequate and impermanent (178–205).

In his ecclesiology, Boff emphasizes that the Incarnation has consequences for the present-day not only in the Christologically interpretative social actions of Christians and Christian communities but also in the sacramental life of the Church. The sacraments, especially the Eucharist, are the seeds of the Resurrection planted in the Church that begin to transform the community into the likeness of the resurrected Christ. While the presence of God in the form of Christ is not limited to the Church's sacramental life—it is to be found in the cosmos as well as in the lives of suffering and oppressed people and in efforts to alleviate pain and liberate from captivity—that presence is most concentrated there (221–25).

The presence of God in our world in the form of Christ should not be thought of, for Boff, as static. The categories of his Christology are dynamic, historical. There is, he insists, a future-oriented quality to our being in the world. Christ may be regarded as the mysterious, inexhaustible presence in that process which can direct the world toward the goal of full relation with the Creator. The liberating activity of the Church, then, should be directed toward that goal. The model is global. The structures of interest, power, and identity that limit societies and human beings should be subverted in the name of this future, a future in which the Church already can participate. Liberation is, then, a positive and not a negative act. It anticipates the new order that will displace the old structures of exclusion, separation, and oppression (247–63).

Boff's Christology has as its central starting point the presence or availability of the divine in our world. Boff's emphasis on the life of Jesus, the sacramental life of the Church, and the communal lives of Christians gives a specific answer, a street address, so to speak, to the question "Where is God?" He supports this specificity of presence against the possible dominance of "x" matters by implying that Christians who are principally concerned about transcendence will be distracted from the actual circumstances of our world to which the Church, as a continuing incarnation, is related and to and for which the Church speaks and acts. While his categories are dynamic and temporal, there is ample "presence" talk to ensure that the Church will not be so concerned with God as to ignore the relation of God to the specific conditions of real people in actual situations.

While he employs social, political, and economic categories to describe the kind of specificity that God's presence in the world takes on, Boff does not allow "z" interests to dominate his Christology. He sets up a contrary relation between the presence of God in the world and the powers, interests, and categories of that world (272). He ties "z" interests to structures and identities that exclude. The humanity of Jesus counters that world and is not articulated with notions about the human that are taken from general anthropological observations. His Christology challenges them, particularly his assertion that Jesus had no personality structure (241). He subordinates "z" to "y" matters by insisting that we do not know the humanity of Jesus from our knowledge of human nature but, rather, that the humanity of Jesus presents to us an entirely different way of being human, a way that challenges worldly assumptions.

III

Hans Küng's ecclesiology also has as its central point the form of God's presence in our world. That presence is the Church's essence, and it makes the Church both constant and historical. This means that the Church, while always identifiable, is also continually changing. The first danger to avoid, according to Küng, is to make too much of the external characteristics of the Church, and both supporters and detractors of the Church do this, those who are impressed by the geographical and historical breadth of the Church, its solemnity and cultural achievements, as well as those who object to its political power, its ritualism, and its dogmatism.[3]

This does not mean that Küng's external/internal distinction resembles the distinction Calvin made between the visible and the invisible Church. The form and essence, even the true and the falsifying aspects of the Church, are interwoven. What in the Church is true and essential belongs as much to the visible as to the invisible, as do also what in the Church is temporary or mistaken (24).

The local church, while it is not the same as *the* Church, also represents it in its entirety. The local church is not a subsection of the Church, but all that the Church is or can become is present in the individual church. One can, in effect, point to a specific location in answer to the question, "Where can God be found?" However, the presence of God in the Church is not identical with all that the Church is.

To clarify this relation, Küng, like Boff, uses dynamic rather than static language. The Church is Church when it is gathered. It is a pilgrim community, *en route*. The Kingdom of God is coming, and the Church is its anticipatory sign. The Church is not an entity situated above or apart from people; it is an actual historical people. Küng prefers the description of the Church as the people of God, a temporal characterization, to that of the body of Christ, a spatial metaphor. "People of God" not only qualifies the spatial with the temporal, it also affects the theology of ecclesiastical offices. Küng moves from the people to the clergy and, finally, to the Pope. It is not as though the essence of the Church rested in the papal office and extended downward to the people (147–201).

The sacraments join the people of God to one another and, in the Eucharist primarily, to Christ, who gives himself in this form to the community. Christ *becomes* present in the Sacrament by the power of Word. The relation of the presence to the elements of the Sacrament is again for Küng dynamic. He wants a sacramental language that will emphasize actuality while still being nonliteral. The relation of Christ to the elements, like his relation to the Church more generally, is neither physical nor merely symbolic. It is a relationship of a common destiny. Without the Church, Christ would not be present to the world, but Christ is not identical with or confined to the Church (275–89).

Such marks of the Church as its unity and catholicity are not primarily organizational, geographical, statistical, or historical concepts. While the Church *is* one, it also must *become* one. That process or event arises from below and not from above. Unity affirms diversity, while each individual church points beyond itself to the whole Church even though what belongs to the whole can be found in each. The Church is a representative community not only to but also of the world (341–411).

Küng seems particularly uneasy with "holy" as a characteristic of the Church. He stresses that evil in the Church is not merely an occasional or superficial matter. "Holy" functions as a temporal term, then; the Church becomes holy by use and service. Objects and places are not holy. Only people can be holy, and they become so by God's use of them (411–43).

Consistent with the whole of his ecclesiology, Küng minimizes the distinction between clergy and laity. One does not precede the other; they are equal in their common subjection to Christ. The sacramental life of the Church is communal and not in the hands of the clergy. That some administer the Sacrament and others do not is more a practical than a theological distinction for Küng. It is more important, for Küng, that the idea of apostolic succession should call attention to ministry for all members of the Church than that it should separate and elevate a group of clergy. Ordination is a call to ministry on behalf of and within the community. It suggests closer identity with the community rather than separation from it (443–95). Küng views the hierarchy of the Church as a more historical than theological matter. It is not to be denied, because the historical life of the Church is an expression of its essence, but it is also not to be identified with the essence of the Church, because it is also the result of human initiative and design. At times the episcopacy and papacy have done the Church important service. For example, during times of political turmoil, churches can maintain relations with one another even though they may be on contrary sides of a political conflict or apart from it. Without the hierarchy of the Church there would have been more fragmentation and more subjection of churches to local political and social interests than is now the case. But the Church is not derived from the bishops and the Pope; they are derived from the Church. They do not represent dominion but service. They are not heads but hands. The authority of these offices arises from their actions and fruits and does not inhere statically within them. The Pope should be called a servant or pastor rather than "head of the church" (566–611). While excesses of authority and power continually appear, these excesses are not exclusive to the Roman Catholic church. They are also to be found in the Orthodox church's attitude toward "tradition," the Protestants' toward the Bible, and the independent churches toward their preachers (609).

The starting point and focus of Küng's ecclesiology is the presence of God in the world by means of the Church, although the Church is defined in dynamic ways and is characterized by incompleteness and even negative aspects as well as by positive. This means that Küng's ecclesiology does not sharply separate the Church from the world or elevate it above a world deemed secular and profane. Küng treats the worldly context of the Church more favorably as potential (not anonymous) Church, and he lays the blame for the secularization of Western culture as much on the Church's attempts, in the Middle Ages, to ecclesiasticize the culture as on the desire of people to reject what the Church really is. Secularization is also a response to excesses within the Church (616–20). Küng's ecclesiology, while it makes "y" interests dominant, is underdeveloped polemically because it is a discourse operating in an ecumenical context and with ecumenical aims. The capacity of "y" elements to discredit the other two kinds is held in check. Underdevelopment and caution of this kind are bound to create impatience among "Y" spokespersons more concerned than Küng to do justice to the dominant of this kind of theology.

IV

The commotion caused among some Catholic theologians by the recent work of Cardinal Joseph Ratzinger can be illuminated in this context. Ratzinger, at one time associated with the Catholic theological left, was one of the founders of *Concilium* in 1964 and could be grouped with Küng as well as with Rahner, Congar, and Schillebeeckx in a circle of ecumenically minded theologians and strong supporters of Vatican II. He seems, now, to have turned, in the direction of his thought, sharply to the right and to be taking positions contrary to the spirit of Vatican II. I would say that he is attempting to grant Catholic theology more coherence and a sharper identity by acting on the capacity for domination inherent to "y" interests.

While there may be many personal, institutional, and political aspects to this change and the tensions it has created between Ratzinger and both his former associates and those young Catholic theologians who take their cues from Vatican II, the point to be observed is that the power of his polemic arises theologically from the potentials for dominance in "y" matters that are not as fully actualized by such Catholic theologians as Boff and Küng. Reading Ratzinger's latest work, whether directly under his name or in the Instructions of the Congregation for the Doctrine of the Faith, in which his influence can clearly be seen, one can see actualized more fully and quite effectively the potential in "y" interests to dominate and to discredit "x" and "z" matters. Ratzinger is reacting to the modification of "y" matters in the work of liberal Catholic theologians whose concern for the other two kinds, for "x" matters, as can be seen in Küng, and for "z" matters, as may be seen in liberation theologies like Boff's, has led them to temper their support of "y" dominance. Ratzinger's response to modification of the Küng type is to insist, for example, that priests are consecrated for "contact with God," that they "approach God," and "with impure hands lay hold on the Untouchable One, the Pure One, the Infinite."[4] This is quite straightforward "presence" talk, and it discredits the metaphors that render "presence" elusive and dynamic in Küng's ecclesiology. For Ratzinger, "presence" requires a particularly designated priesthood, specifically one in the apostolic succession. This grants to clergy unique powers and privileges as well as responsibilities. His response to the accommodation of "z" matters takes several forms but none more provocative than in his reservations concerning the social and political orientation of liberation theology, such as provided by the example of Boff. He is uneasy about the Church's endorsement of social, political, and economic interests, and he wants to keep in place the Church's sense of distinction from the secular world. What appears to be good, obvious, and logical in the world is always tainted by the "spirit" of the world, and the Church must always be nonconforming to it.[5]

It is not my purpose to say how Catholic theologians or, even more, the Church should move in this quite heated polemical situation. Nor am I taking sides. Rather, I want only to point out that Ratzinger's recent moves produce a theological discourse that is more intensely "priestly" than Boff's or Küng's and that this kind of discourse has been more consistent than theirs with the Church's sense of identity and practice, especially since the rise of Protestant communities. For these two reasons, but especially because of the integrity of priestly discourses, the ability, that is, of "y" to dominate "x" and "z" and deform them to itself, Ratzinger's reaction to the less than full development of priestly discourse among liberal Catholic theologians will have considerable *theological*—along with institutional and political—power.

Priestly discourse will not disappear from the theological forum even in the unlikely event that the theological orientation of *Concilium* were to become that of the Church more widely. Indeed, I began this discussion with the Christology of a Protestant. Unfortunately, however, priestly discourse, when it becomes explicit concerning the nature of Scripture in conservative Protestant circles or implicit in the appeals of the "kingdoms" announced by TV evangelists, seems to lack the rich context of attitudes toward "presence" that marks Catholic piety, liturgy, and institutions.

6

SAPIENTIAL DISCOURSES

A HIDDEN PREMISE IN THEOLOGICAL discourses of the third type is that the needs and potentials of the human world form the starting point and focus of attention. This starting point carries as much capacity for dominance as do "y" and "x" matters, and starting with the needs and potentials of the human world has all the force of the obvious. Sapiential theologians will assume that, since we live in a world with real potentials and needs, it is in and for that world that theology should be done. In polemic they will suggest the life-denying obscurantism and privatization of the other discourses. They will point out how imperialistic or irrelevant to human life discourses of the other types tend to be.

While discourses of this kind will begin with a close attention to the needs and potentials of the human world they will differ from one another in many ways. One point of difference will be in the assessment of the value, reliability, or accessibility of the social and "natural" world in which we are living. Not all sapiential theology is optimistic or sanguine, and it is a mistake to assume that theologies with negative appraisals of human life are thereby prophetic or priestly. True, there is an almost unavoidable affirmation in this kind of theology of the human capacity for observation and reflection, but these activities can lead to widely differing assessments. This point is worth making because sapiential theologies have made adjustments to the change in evaluation of the human enterprise that came about in the modern period due to rapid industrialization, colonization, urban expansion, and, most of all, the First World War. Sapiential theologies have become more critical and pessimistic concerning the human enterprise.

A more important distinction to be made among sapiential theologies has to do with direction or orientation. I identify three principal options here, three foci that are distinguishable from one another. The first of these orientations is the human world in its natural aspect. This stress can, philosophically, take an ontological or a cosmological form. But it need not be directed only to such interests. The "natural" can also be an internal or personal matter, whether individually or communally construed. Or it can have as its focus such "natural" moments in human experience as spontaneity or a sense of relation to the preconscious extensions of the conscious life. This first orientation relates human life to its natural context, environment, or sources as providing moral and spiritual guidance or renewal.

A second group of sapiential theologies can be designated as those concerned with differences and relations among humans, especially the problems and possibilities of human societies. This set of interests is directed to the conflicts within particular societies, to the relations between social groups, and to questions of differences and mutual understanding among people. In interests of this kind attention is given to the problem for human societies created by differences among people, and the potential affirmed is the enrichment and enlargement of life that is available through an appreciation and affirmation of diversity.

A final orientation of sapiential theologies is toward a transcendent whole that provides human life a direction for its present course. This is the more "spiritual" side of sapiential theology. It depicts that sense of unity for which human beings do or ought to yearn, a possibility that, while it lies always beyond human grasp, is yet also an aspect of experience or an object of religious imagination. It is a principle or power of unity or completion that lies, somehow, above or ahead of the human enterprise.

The traditional theological topics that form the starting point and primary interest of sapiential discourses are theological anthropology and soteriology, the understanding, that is, of human needs and potentials and of how these needs can be answered or those potentials actualized. But these two topics are even more intertwined in sapiential theologies than are Christology and ecclesiology in priestly and theology and eschatology in prophetic. Therefore, it seems better to treat my examples along the lines of the threefold distinction I suggested than to use the two traditional categories or foci.

Prophetic and priestly discourses are also interested in anthropology and soteriology, although these topics will be dominated by and deformed towards the principal power and meaning points in those respective discourses, and sapiential discourses are interested in "x" and "y" matters, although they are subjected to the primacy of "z." In sapiential discourses the form or occasion of divine presence in the world, then, is not likely to be a specific time, place, object, institution, or person but, rather, general ontological, sociological, or spiritual conditions and occasions. Primarily the form or occasion of "x" is the created order, moments in individual or communal human experiences, or that which is beyond us, for which we yearn and reach or by which our endeavors are completed or lured.

The biblical texts that form the precedent for theology of this kind are, of course, the wisdom materials, products of various kinds that arise from the circles of sages. This means not only the wisdom books—Proverbs, Job, and Ecclesiastes, for example—but also several Psalms and many biblical narratives.

Biblical wisdom provides a moral and spiritual orientation that has its origin and principal focus neither in the power and prerogatives of deity nor in the authority of sacred times, places, and objects; rather, it is based on the problems and potentials of human experience. A principal source for the sapiential theologies of our own day must be thought of as the Old Testament, although some aspects of the New Testament Gospels and books such as the Epistle of James can be included. But by their very nature, sapiential interests, whether in ancient Israel or in modern times, are open to contributions from other cultures because of the orientation in this kind of discourse to various human needs, potentials, and experiences.

The three emphases or orientations of sapiential theologies can be found in biblical wisdom. First, the wise person is continually called on to observe and to be corrected by the natural world. Nature is not employed simply to reinforce or to illustrate moral teachings. Rather, it is invoked for its power to correct the follies and distortions to which people are prone. The wise person is fascinated by natural surroundings, and Solomon, it is written, "spoke of trees, from the cedar that is in Lebanon to the hyssop that grows out of the wall; he spoke also of beasts, and of birds, and of reptiles, and of fish." The wise person is related to a natural world that grants steadiness, simplicity, and moral health.

One also finds in the wisdom literature that the resolution of social conflicts receives major attention. The wisdom movement may have gained prominence when Israel first developed mature relations with other nations. Wisdom was an international and cosmopolitan phenomenon. Solomon is inscribed as a person of shrewd judgment, able to interpret subtle interpersonal conflicts. The wise person is one who is sensitive to the conflicts between various cultures but also to tensions within society, complex relations between men and women, the young and the elderly, and the individual and the group.

The third characteristic of the wise person is an orientation to a transcendent image of completion and coherence. This image is found in the opening chapters of Proverbs, where wisdom is personified in a feminine form. Although the interpretation of this figure in Jewish and Christian traditions is complex, it seems clear that wisdom is a principle of perfection that is both fascinating to and unattainable by human beings but one toward which the wise person aspires.

The examples of sapiential theology that I have selected are all American. This is not the place to elaborate on the special importance of sapiential discourses for the formation of American culture, but it is possible to say, I think, that American theology of the twentieth century is largely known for its anthropological orientation. This is no simple oddity. While from the Puritans on there have been prophetic discourses of great importance in America, and while both Catholic and Protestant discourses of a priestly nature continue to have their impact, the major strand of American theology is sapiential. The examples I shall use, therefore, are domestic, and this shift will balance the heavily foreign direction of my attention in the previous chapters.

I

The three examples I have chosen of the first kind of sapiential theology, namely, that which is directed to the need for human life to be related to its "natural" context, are quite separable from one another as to what they take the natural to be or mean. William James, Henry Nelson Wieman, and Bernard Meland, while they can be placed in a particular stream of American theological anthropology and soteriology, have very different points to make. By beginning with James, who cannot so readily be identified as a Christian theologian as can most of the others treated in this section, I want to emphasize the continuity that exists between Christian theology and anthropological and soteriological discourses more generally conceived.

James takes human experience as his starting point. Since an experience is of something, religious experience points beyond itself. When forced to say what this something is, James calls it the "more," and he relates it to the subconscious continuation of our conscious life. He finds it possible to move from this "more" to the "over-belief" in a divine power when he appeals to the results of such a belief.[1] Religion, for James, is to be advocated not because of its roots and certainly not because of its absolutes but because of its fruits (35 and 261). The principal fruit of belief in a divine power is to grant an underlying sense of confidence in the universe. In order to have that sense of confidence, faith in the power of the unseen reality is necessary (58).

In addition to feeling at home in the universe, a person also needs to feel unified. A second fruit of belief is the unification of the self. This involves primarily a union between the conscious and the subconscious parts of the person. A person of faith does not have fear of or distance from the subconscious (397).

Finally, the person of faith has a unified moral life and integrity. The "sand and grit," the "disorder and slackness, and vague superfluity" of a person's life dissolve (225 and 238). Unity of action joins the other two, unity with the subconscious extension of the conscious life and unity with the universe, to form the fruits of belief.

Religious experiences and beliefs vary much, for James, and the unseen reality, the divine, or God is not authoritatively experienced in any one religious form. Each articulation constitutes a syllable in a larger message about God, and only the whole of humanity can begin to spell out its meaning (379). In addition, religious pluralism is inevitable, given the variety of human constitutions, the variety of human types. This point accounts for his well-known distinctions between the healthy-minded, of both the involuntary and the systematic kinds, and the sick-souls.

Belief is not only a gift, for James; it can also be willed. We may at times be called on to decide whether or not to believe even though we would prefer to wait until more information is in. Some very basic questions concerning human life cannot wait for answers until enough information is in. I must decide, for example, whether my actions do or do not make a difference in the world or whether or not my life is worth living. James contends that it is better to believe that my actions have meaning and my life has value, because such beliefs create a climate in which I will act and will experience meaning and value. A person's beliefs are constitutive elements in what that person experiences.[2]

Furthermore, for James, beliefs of this kind may well correspond to the actual state of affairs ontologically. The world in which we live is emerging and pluralistic. This means that our actions may make a difference, however small, in the direction that process takes. Commitment to a possibility in an open universe is no futile exercise.[3]

James stresses the primacy of religious experience, belief, and human needs and potentials at the expense of the claims of "y" matters. He has little interest in the authority of ecclesiastical structures or in religious objects for their own sake. He takes formalized or institutionalized religion as a product of the reality he takes as authoritative, namely, individual religious experiences (41 and 267). And he subjects "x" matters to his starting point by treating the divine as the objective aspect of human belief and as what humans need in order to feel at home in the universe. People possess the potential for experiencing the divine (48).

The starting point of James's religious anthropology, then, is the need and potential in human life for connection and wholeness, connection with the subconscious continuation of conscious life and with the universe, and wholeness both of life style and of a sense of the world in which humans live. His assessment of human needs and potentials determines what James has to say about "x" matters, the transcendent or divine, and about "y" matters, the availability of the divine in the human world.

In the work of Henry Nelson Wieman theological anthropology is done in the context of neonaturalism. However much Wieman was influenced by the process thought of Whitehead and associated with Charles Hartshorne, he turned away from metaphysics and directed his interest in process philosophy toward theological anthropology and soteriology. His primary attention is given to the human propensity for evil and the possibility that humans can be transformed in ways they cannot transform themselves.[4] The basic category for Wieman is not experience, as with James, but event. For Wieman human beings need to be changed, delivered from their own propensity to sin and from the consequences of evil around them. This requires an event that is not of their own making. This special kind of event, one that lies beyond human design and control and that transforms people as they need to be transformed and cannot transform themselves, is called "creative good."[5]

While creative good is concentrated, as far as we can observe, in human relations, it is not simply an aspect or dimension of human life. Rather, it transcends human intention and understanding, although it does not transcend the time and space world with which human beings are identified (264). Here Wieman places more emphasis on "x" matters than James, for the event of creative interchange cannot be a matter of will, as the transforming power of belief is for James, but is gratuitous. He also has a more articulated interest in "y" matters, for God is not identified with the emergent, pluralistic universe, as in James, but takes the form of specific, separable moments in human relationships. However, while saying this it should also be made clear that for Wieman "x" and "y" matters are strongly subjected to and left deformed toward his principal interest in human moral and spiritual needs and potentials.

More of a Christian theologian than James, Wieman points to biblical moments in which God in the form of creative interchange is present in the world of human relations. He sees in the relation of Jesus to his disciples a manifestation of this event and its accompanying subevents. When Jesus died, the hopes of his disciples died with him. But in the resurrection something unexpected occurred. The disciples perceived a new meaning that changed their understandings of themselves, one another, and the world; the event created a new community. This event epitomizes and clarifies those transforming events that Wieman designates as creative interchange. Such events release people from an already existent value and graft them in new relationships both to other people and to their environment (43–44).

The human world, then, is constantly being renewed for Wieman by a God present to it in creative, transforming events, and it is the role of human beings to trust and be open to them. The reality of these events, open to public identification, grants an objectivity to value that delivers it from moral relativism, from the notion that value is a matter of individual taste and preference. The power and truth of the divine, he believes, are open to public experience and verification (181–90).

For Wieman the neonaturalist, creative events can be said to arise from below rather than descend from above, if such spatial language can be added to the temporal categories he prefers. With Wieman one can adumbrate the work of a number of American theologians who at one time or another have had a noticeable impact—Sam Keen, Richard Rubenstein, Harvey Cox, Donald Schon, Herbert Richardson, Tom Driver, and David Miller. Theirs are gods from below, too, and the saving event is a matter of release from confinement or distortion and of participation in natural potentials that lead a person or a group from a situation of need to transformation and fulfillment.

Bernard Meland adds a distinctive and major theological note because of his orientation to the social sciences, particularly cultural anthropology. It is Meland's principal concern to speak of religious life in relation to mediating historical, cultural, and mythic influences by which humans are formed as individuals in real and primary relations to other individuals and to their social and historical environments generally.[6]

He carries on this work in open objection to the liberal tradition in Protestant theology that considers access to God as primarily an affair of reason and that looks to consciousness as "the highest exemplification of spiritual good" (125). In fact, Meland does not hesitate to identify this isolation and elevation of the rational self as the arrogance and "hardening" of sin. This criticism he carries on from insights provided by scientific and social scientific work of this century, insights that lead to what he calls a "holistic view of the human situation," a view that takes as primary "the relational aspect of man's existence and the depth of meaning" upon which conscious life depends.[7]

The guidelines that he follows for the development of a post- or antiliberal sapiential theology are emphases on depth, emergence, and the power of myth and intuition. While Meland emphasizes the continuity of the work or even the presence of God with everyday human affairs, an emphasis that allows for an empirical approach, he stresses even more events that transform human life and create relations in ways for which humans cannot claim credit.[8] The "depth" of which he speaks is not so much "under" us as "behind" us in the rich and meaningful resources that emerge in every moment, past attitudes and acts that people at any moment are incapable of exhausting or of fully comprehending (103–5). And myth and intuition refer to the hidden psychic shapes or structures that relate communities and individuals to the meaningfulness that underlies conscious life, that accounts, say, for occasions that suddenly bring tears to one's eyes, whether of joy or sorrow (143).

The response of a community, or of a person in that community, to all of this should be one of faith, that is, of a relation to or openness toward it, a prereflective, prearticulated relation of trust toward life. "Depth and a dynamic power of renewal, then, are the two dimensions that faith imparts to culture and to the individual life" (15).

Although it is more than this, Meland's category of faith is primarily a kind of epistemology, and he speaks most often of it as appreciative awareness, an attitude that allows knowledge to arise from relationship and wonder, of understanding as resting on "a depth of feeling, signs, and symbolic utterances which exemplify resources of meaningfulness even when they cannot, on technical [that is, philosophical or scientific] grounds, be said to have meaning" (82). Faith seeks and gives rise to understanding.

One of the more problematic categories in Meland's position is "culture," which is roughly analogous for a community to what personality is for an individual. It both forms and is formed by the community; it is both good and evil; and it is both continuous with and resistive to God's acting. Culture carries the results of revelation in concrete ways. It is the structure of related meanings in which the nature of God's working must be felt and expressed, and it prepares a people for revelation. On the other hand, "the current culture in any period of history in the form of men's acts, their desires, institutions, and policies, may be a betrayal of what is deepest in the cultural inheritance" (101).

The revelation of God, to be seen for our culture primarily in the redemptive act of Christ, is that persuasive and re-creative force of love, forgiveness, and healing that Meland calls the "tenderness of life" (126). Although the relation of this force to what he refers to as the brute forces is not altogether clear, Meland chooses to speak of God's work as primarily effecting, so to speak, meltings of ice between human beings, of what keeps people from appreciative awareness of their relations to one another and to the prereflective meaning by which they are formed. This work of God, this good that is not of our own collective or individual making, can produce in people a "sense of otherness as a real, defining, even assertive dimension of man's existence."[9]

The "y" and "x" matters, although they are granted considerable distinctiveness in Meland's theology, are subordinated to "z." The form or occasion of God's presence in the world, the "y" matter, for Meland is a prevenient meaning that forms the substructure of human life, nurtures human relations, and certifies values. God, or the "x" component of his theology, while not separable from the human world, is certainly not identical with powers of consciousness by which humans understand and determine their lives and world. Indeed, God seems as much to counter, to judge, human self-determination as to support or legitimate it. God is related to the human environment by which humans are created and nurtured and of which they are not and never can be fully comprehending or even aware.

II

My reading of the above three sapiential theologies construes their theological anthropology and soteriology in terms of the human need and potential for a relation to the natural context of life, however differently among the three that context is described. I turn now to discourses directed to the second principal sapiential interest—societies and their complexities. Again, the examples, while having this orientation in common, differ sharply from one another.

Walter Rauschenbusch, one such theologian, sees in Christianity unique possibilities for overcoming social divisions and moving toward social unity. He finds in contemporary American democracy an opportunity for Christianity to achieve a mission given to it by the ministry of Jesus but heretofore unrealizable. The great stretch of Christian history from the life of Jesus to the present time has been marked by the unfortunate reinforcement of social division by Christian institutions and thought. Theology in modern America has the unique opportunity of reviving the message that God, immanent in social history, provides the means for a reconciliation between people now separated from one another.[10] He envisions this unity not only within but between social groups, for humanity itself is a great solidarity within which God himself dwells (97). That which resists or distrusts this unity is evil, and the chief cause of resistance and distrust is preoccupation with self or one's own group (50–51). Redemption is actually a process of incorporation within ever enlarging groups, into societies that resemble families. The seed of social wholeness that Christianity spreads, for Rauschenbusch, has fallen on no more fertile ground than that of modern American democracy.

Rauschenbusch's strong interest in biblical prophets does not yield a "prophetic" quality to his own work. His principal interest in the prophets is in the egalitarian and humanitarian emphasis of their messages and not in their appeal to the terrible power and primacy of Yahweh. The prophetic denunciation of greed and pride that separate and elevate some people at the expense of others—this is a prophetic emphasis immediately useful to Rauschenbusch. In fact, he attacks "x" interests by arguing that an emphasis on the power, transcendence, unpredictability, and primacy of God finds support in hierarchical political and ecclesiastical structures (170). People took notions of divinity from the style and position of kings and governors, turning God into an autocrat. Christianity is stuck with a view of God wholly inappropriate to the rise of democracy. What is needed is a recognition that God is immanent in humanity, particularly manifest in moments when people who differ from one another join one another for the common good. The basis for such moments is God, for God is "the ground for the spiritual oneness of the race and of our hope for its close fellowship in the future" (186).

Rauschenbusch subjects "y" to "z" claims in his discourse by contending that the Kingdom of God is not identified with the boundaries of the Church and its activities but embraces the whole of human life. The Church errs by creating a separation between itself and society; it errs by directing attention to otherworldly possibilities rather than to needs and potentials within the social order; and the Church errs by easily generating airs of authority and uniqueness. There are, for Rauschenbusch, only two kinds of theology, one that arises from and supports the privilege of ruling groups and despots and one that affirms and supports democracy (144–45). For Rauschenbusch God is actually present in the growth of democracy, and the Church, if it presses its uniqueness into authoritative models, will simply lose its sense of or participation in the presence and work of God altogether.

Reinhold Niebuhr, a second theologian of this type, is as much opposed to the individualism of Protestant theological anthropology in America as is Rauschenbusch, but he lacks Rauschenbusch's optimism concerning the form of social life in this country for two reasons. First, groups are not better than individuals; they are generally worse. They are less reasonable, less aware of others, and less self-critical than individuals.[11] Change must be effected in groups primarily by power. And rather than moving toward greater unity within themselves and between one another, social groups are always beset by internal and external conflicts. Social division is a permanent condition (6–10).

A second reason for Niebuhr's pessimistic view of the human social situation is that social conflicts attach themselves to contraries in human life that seem to be unavoidable and irremediable. The human world is divided not only by social, historical, and economic conditions and interactions but also by constitution, by nature. Endemic to the human situation are contraries that are always causing and aggravating social division and conflict. The contrariness of human nature, both individual and social, defeats all attempts to comprehend it and to believe in its eventual amelioration.[12] Much of Niebuhr's work, therefore, is devoted to exposing the partialities and inadequacies of existing theological and philosophical anthropologies in dealing with those contraries (26–54).

The divisions and contraries in human life do not only cause evils, however; they are also responsible for corrections and for good. History is characterized wholly, therefore, by neither one nor the other. Because of the divisions in life, there can be criticism, correction, and vision. Human life is tragic but not desperate, incomplete but not meaningless (263).

While he is often read as what I call a "prophetic" theologian, Niebuhr, in my opinion, allows "z" matters to dominate "x" by moving to a discussion of God *from* his analysis of human nature and history. In this regard he is very different from "prophetic" theologians. Although often thought of as the American neoorthodox theologian, Niebuhr's emphases are different from Barth's and those associated with Barth's orientation. True, Niebuhr shares with Barth a dim view of the human enterprise, but his understanding of God is more derived from his analysis of the human situation than the other way around. There is actual good and meaning in human history because God is present in and to it. "The eternal is the ground and source of the temporal. The divine consciousness gives meaning to the mere succession of natural events by comprehending them simultaneously, even as human consciousness gives meaning to segments of natural sequence by comprehending them simultaneously in memory and foresight."[13] The model Niebuhr uses to describe the relation of God to human history is an anthropological one. It is the model of what for him is the nature of man, composed of contraries especially along the lines of sensual and spiritual characteristics. The transcendence of God is homologous to the self-transcendence of the person and the (dimmer) possibilities of self-transcendence in social groups. Despite their great differences, Niebuhr's work can more appropriately be grouped with Rauschenbusch's as an example of sapiential discourse than with Barth's as an example of prophetic. He differs from Rauschenbusch less in starting point than in his estimation of that starting point. While he has a more complicated and negative view of human history and society than Rauschenbusch, he also does his theology from a dominant "z" position.

Niebuhr's theology subjects "y" to "z" interests by treating the Church as subject to the divisive conditions that characterize the human situation. So, for example, the difference between Catholic and Protestant churches can be construed in terms of the contraries that mark human interests generally. What is more, Niebuhr, while with wholly different purposes, can be as critical of the pretentions of the Church as can prophetic theologians. Sapiential discourses can make common polemical cause against religious institutions with prophetic. Niebuhr is well known for his criticism of the irrelevance, self-indulgence, and pride of the churches. Religion tends to absolutize the group, to be ideology that favors advantage.[14] His treatment of ecclesiology as well as Christology is enfolded within the general analysis of human nature and history.

A third example of a sapiential discourse directed to social dynamics and cultural conflicts can be found in a text by Langdon Gilkey. *Naming the Whirlwind* counters neoorthodox, speculative, and radical Protestant theology with a theological anthropology derived from an analysis of moments and dimensions of human experience, on the one hand, and the history of religious language available to society, on the other. The gap or division in contemporary human life lies exactly here, between experience and religious language.[15]

Gilkey tries to bring these two sides of contemporary society together by pointing out that secular people are more religious and religious people more secular than they suppose themselves to be. He sees the modern problem, the break between experiences and a language employable to interpret them, as due to our unreadiness to talk openly and frankly about experiences of ultimacy and depth common to us all. Because we refrain from talk of this kind, the common arena is impoverished and its language bereft of the resources adequate to such experience (31–40).

The avoidance of reference to experiences of depth and ultimacy grants to secular language a kind of certainty and finality it should not be allowed to have. Meanwhile, our traditional religious languages become increasingly isolated from the common and daily life. The "religious" is turned into a segment removed from the whole, and the truly revelatory dimensions of experience become closed to it. The goal of his work, then, is to uncover the possible unity that can exist between experience and religious language (444). In the latter stages of his argument Gilkey turns explicitly to Paul Tillich's theology of correlation; human experience creates the problems and questions while the tradition of religious symbols provides a resource for their answers (454–57). Gilkey's hope for a more human future rests on the theologian's ability to adumbrate a fruitful, mutually illuminating relation between the now separated depths of human experience and society's inherited religious language.

The "x" interests in this discourse are clearly subjected to Gilkey's anthropological agenda. Talk about the divine, he argues, should be determined by its appearance to us in finite things and events, in the midst of our lives as "contingent, temporal, and autonomous beings." Theology is "talk about creatures, others and ourselves, as the sacred appears to them" (465).

The particular forms of divine presence in Christ, Church, or Scripture are dissolved by Gilkey into a general category of religious symbols. Such terms as "Creator," "Provider," and "Savior" begin to take on new meaning when their relation to experiences of ultimacy and depth in supposedly "secular" experience is made clear (456). "Doctrines take their shape as answers to the problems uncovered by an analysis of secular existence" (457). Clearly, "y" matters in this discourse are being deformed, no less than "x" matters, toward the dominant interest in human needs and potentials.

These three theologians, Rauschenbusch, Niebuhr, and Gilkey, while very different from one another, provide examples of sapiential discourses directed to historical, social, and cultural aspects of the human world. The evils of human society and history in each case are division and conflict, and the aim in each is to uncover the possibilities of unity and wholeness in or for human society and culture. While the sources and forms of conflict and of unity or wholeness differ among them, the principal orientation of their discourses is remarkably similar.

III

The third direction of American sapiential anthropology and soteriology is not so much downward toward the "natural" context or continuation of human life nor outward toward the complexities and dynamics of human society and culture but upward toward the completion of human life in or by some ideal or transcendent principle. It is oriented to or by an image of unity or perfection toward which humans aspire but cannot fully grasp. It rests on the affirmation that the incompleteness and incoherence of human life find their completion and resolution in an elevated, even transcendent, whole. The texts I have chosen are by Josiah Royce, H. Richard Niebuhr, and Shubert Ogden.

Royce's *The Problem of Christianity* is a theology of interpretation. Royce uses as his starting point an impasse that has been reached by the relation of contemporaries to their Christian history; the enlightened mind finds Christianity unacceptable. This impasse calls for interpretation, a creative effort to find some resolution above the two parties—the contemporary intellectual situation and Christian theology—by which each will find its chief interests served, a point that is not so much a compromise or a mixture but a compound, a new thing.[16]

This work of interpretation *must* occur because it is in this way that history is created, both personal and communal. Every self is actually an interpretation, a compound constituted of diverse factors and providing a coherent whole. Communities, like individual selves, also must constantly be interpreting the past to their present in order to have a future. Communities and selves are interpretations in time, and the two are involved in one another because much of a person's history is communal as well as individual.[17] This interpretative activity *can* fruitfully be undertaken because the newly created whole that is the product of interpretation always already exists for Royce. Wherever genuine interpretation occurs, it has been adumbrated by the Spirit of the Community of Interpretation, which is always adding to its enduring domain. All interpretations are housed by this transcendent whole.[18]

People constantly find themselves in predicaments that depend on acts of interpretation for their healing. This is caused, among other things, by the process of increasing self-consciousness, principally the awareness of oneself as an object in the field of another's awareness. A state of tension exists, then, between the social and individual aspects of one's own life and between a person as an individual and as part of the collective. This situation will, if nothing is done, degenerate into mutual distrust, into increasing individual*ism* and collectiv*ism*, a crescendoing dissonance of unfruitful alienation. What is needed is a community in which individuals are together not at the price of their individuality but with the actualization of full, individual potential within and for the sake of the community.[19] The community is more than the sum of its members, then; it is the coincidence of many individual contributions constituting a new thing, a thing that would not exist without the contributions of all the members.

The natural evil of an individual's inevitable alienation from the communal aspect of his or her own life is not the only kind of evil that the ideal community, the new thing, must overcome. There are also moral evils, acts done against the community, particularly acts of betrayal. Such evils can be overcome by events that provide a sublation of the former state, a reconstitution of the community that could not have been realized had the act of betrayal not been committed. Such acts turn betrayal into a *felix culpa* (308–10 and 319–20).

Interpretation for Royce, then, is the principal human act, distinct from perceptions and conceptions, addressing the major human need for healing the tragic tensions within and among people. The human world can be restored when interpretation, based on the faith that our interpreting efforts are not in vain because we are being interpreted, overcomes acts of betrayal against the community with acts of rectitude that grant atonement (271–323).

Royce finds his theories of the Community of Interpretation expressed in the New Testament, particularly in Paul's understanding of the Church, its transcendent unity, its embodiment of the spirit of its founder, and its ability fully to accommodate the contributions of its individual members. Royce does not feel that he is slighting Christianity in his attempts to transcend the impasse of its separation from the modern intellect, for what the present most sorely needs—the Community of Interpretation—is what is also of primary importance for, even the very essence of, early Christianity (79–106).

Although the transcendent is of great importance to the text, as are also Royce's Christological and ecclesiological sections, there is little danger in mistaking Royce for a prophetic or priestly theologian. As to the first, Royce argues the importance of the transcendent from the process of interpretation and not from its own primacy or power. And a more priestly theologian than Royce would argue that the person of the founder is more important and determining for Christianity than are the resources of the community. Although Royce would argue that for the Pauline Christian it is not the founder "after the flesh" that is primary but the spirit of the founder in the community,[20] Royce would be perceived by a priestly theologian as dissolving the particular qualities of the Christian Church into general and universal categories. Royce would counter by saying that Christians already have done this with eschatology; Christians do not generally believe, as did the Pauline churches, in the imminent end of the world. Royce believes his reinterpretation of Christology is similar. Anyone these days who asserts a traditional Christology "involves himself in historical, in metaphysical, in technically theological, and elementally religious problems, which all advances in our modern sciences and in our humanities, in our spiritual life and in our breadth of outlook upon the universe, have only made, for the followers of tradition, constantly harder to face and to solve."[21] The priestly theologian would argue that Royce has elevated standards and criteria drawn from academic and scientific institutions and practices above the authority of "y" matters. Royce's response to the claims of "x" and "y" is that they lead to obscurantism and irrelevance, the very problems for or in Christianity that he, with this "z" discourse, is trying to overcome.

H. Richard Niehubr, a theologian heavily influenced by Josiah Royce, defines the nature and role of faith, of relations of trust and loyalty, in terms of something fundamental to and unavoidable in human life. The question to be raised of a person is not *whether* he or she has faith but toward *what* that faith is directed. In *Radical Monotheism and Western Culture* Niebuhr argues to the transcendent from the needs of faith and from the inadequacies revealed in faiths that do not have the transcendent as their object. The typology he uses to describe kinds of faith comprises "polytheism," "henotheism," and "monotheism."[22] The last of these, which he advocates and relates to Christianity, is clarified in relation to human needs that the other forms of faith do not answer. "Polytheism" is characterized by a variety of faith objects, a valuing, for example, of work, family, art, and a host of others things, activities, or ideas. "Henotheism" comes to expression in a person committed to some particular in the world that is elevated above competitors and to which other concerns are subjected. For the "monotheist," however, the faith relation is not with a being or value that is in the world but with the transcendent source of being and of value (12–13).

"Monotheism" can be distinguished from the other forms of faith because it is a response to revelation and has a radical quality. For the Christian this revelation is primarily available in Christ. In Christ God makes himself known as the one who is faithful and loyal to the person. Radical faith is a response to being valued. Out of a relation of faith the person returns to the world finding all in it and all relations relative to it of potential value. But such faith, while it addresses the human need for faith, slips easily back into henotheism and even into the "despair" of polytheism (53).

While a person knows God only in the faith relation of trust and loyalty to the one who values the person, such a faith relation is not the only kind of awareness of God's presence that people have. As he says, quoting from Whitehead, "Religion is transition from God the void to God the enemy, and from God the enemy to God the companion" (123–24). The awareness of God as void arises out of the sense of emptiness when the vitality of more proximate values dwindles or evaporates. The awareness of God as enemy arises from the recognition that we are so largely determined by the processes and structures of the world we live in, and we are frustrated by these limitations. But when God is recognized as the one who values us and in whom we can have trust, then the God who limits and the God who lies beyond everything changes to the God with whom one works as a responsible self and the God who is the source of all value and being (124–26).

For Niebuhr, then, values arise from relationships of faith. Knowledge, communication, and appreciation are built on right relations, on relations from which good arises. Faith is fundamental to human life. But a misplaced or scattered loyalty is enervating and distressing.

Like Royce, Niebuhr finds the completion, the principal of wholeness and unity, in a transcendent source. He moves to the need for, dependence on, and faith in this reality from an analysis of the human situation as otherwise in states of incoherence and incompleteness. He appeals to Christian forms in their relevance to human needs. The consequent subordination of "y" matters may be clearer than the subjection of "x," since so much is made of the transcendent. However, the transcendent is not a dominant; rather, the transcendent assures that the human needs already described can be met and that human potentials already established can be actualized.

The dominance of interests in the needs and potentials of the human world could not be clearer than it is in Shubert Ogden's work. Theology for Ogden is anthropology, and a theology is untenable when it denies that "statements about God may be interpreted as statements about man."[23] Statements about God must be interpreted "without remainder as statements about human existence" if they are to have any intellectual credibility (153). All theological propositions that have any validity or force turn out to be not about God first of all but "about man and his possibilities of self-understanding" (137).

The principal problem for human life, for Ogden, the center of his theological anthropology, is how it may be possible to affirm the value and meaning of life in spite of "conditions that make for the profoundest uncertainty about what the future finally holds."[24] This matter is basic to religious experience and to theological reflection.

As an answer to it, Ogden does not refer the reader to a particular form of divine presence in the world or even so much to God as the one who responds to the uncertainties of life with the certainties of revelation. Rather, he appeals to the "original confidence in the meaning and worth of life, through which not simply all our religious answers, but even our religious questions first become possible or have any sense" (33–34). This "original confidence" is a given, and Christian theology is primarily a way of understanding and confirming it. The ground or cause of that confidence, which all who use language, for example, have, is God. "God" is the appropriate name of that "objective ground in reality itself of our ineradicable confidence in the final worth of our existence" (37). To live is to have confidence in the worth and meaning of life. Living then becomes an experience of faith or trust in God, for God is that which causes or grounds that confidence.

Belief in God, then, is unavoidable. Ogden argues this neither by calling attention to the force of his logic nor by arriving at God as a required conclusion to a metaphysical description of the structure of our world; he argues it from human experience and from the unavoidability of belief in the trustworthiness of human life, an unavoidability that grants life its wholeness and direction.

This does not mean that people do not encounter threats to that sense of wholeness and direction, even to the fundamental sense of the value of life. We do encounter "limiting" questions, such as whether our actions make any difference, whether things are the way we understand them, or if there are any real reasons why we should be moral. But while such questions threaten the faith that grants life its direction and wholeness, they also clarify that faith. For no logically, metaphysically, or empirically found answers can be forceful and convincing enough to counter them. While faith may be threatened by them, it is, finally, by faith that they must be overcome (33).

Ogden finds most helpful for the articulation of this faith the process philosophies of Whitehead and Charles Hartshorne. The theology that emerges in this articulation depicts God as immanent and relative, as the one who makes human confidence in the future possible and who grants to people the assurance that faith in the final worth of life will not be disappointed (64).

It should be clear how and why Ogden allows "x" matters in his work to be determined by his starting point and central interest in human needs and potentials. It should also be clear how and why "y" interests are subjected in this discourse; the devaluation of "y" matters is apparent in the removal of distinction between sacred and secular, a removal to which all sapiential theologians contribute. Ogden conceives his theology for the secular person as much as for the religious. And the authoritative in his work is not a particular form of revelation or divine presence but the nature of human experience.

IV

These readings of texts by American sapiential theologians reveal basic differences in their anthropologies and soteriologies. Human need and the answer to that need can be described as estrangement from and reconnection with the natural continuation and context of our lives, as the conflicts and tensions among social groups and within human history, and as the incompleteness and incoherence of human experience that finds its fulfillment in principles of unity and wholeness that transcend it. These are, it seems to me, also the principal preoccupations of the biblical wisdom literature, and a fairly solid biblical basis, precedent, or counterpart to modern sapiential theology can be found in that literature.

But because of its peculiar dynamics, sapiential theology does not require biblical legitimation. I offer the biblical precedent or counterpart more so that those oriented to one of the other two types of theology will be prevented from alienating sapiential theologies from the tradition. Sapiential theology is or can be as biblical and traditional as either of the other two kinds.

CONCLUSION

Theology and the Culture of Scripture and Belief

THIS READING OF THEOLOGICAL texts substantiates, it is hoped, the following proposals: 1) that theological discourses are determined by three principal interests; 2) that theological discourses pursue the consequences of a certain arrangement of these interests, particularly that, since one is and should be dominant, the other two cannot and should not be dominant but should be subjected to and deformed toward the dominant interest; and 3) that differing theological discourses conflict with one another both because they challenge the legitimacy of opposing discourses' dominants and the subordinate roles given in opposing discourses to their own dominants and because they defend their own dominants and the subordinate positions to which they relegate the dominants of opposing discourses. The differing arrangements, actual or potential, of the three kinds of language in these discourses is to be counted as the principal focus of theological argumentation. It is hoped that a way of reading has been provided that will distinguish theological discourses from one another and anticipate and recognize the determining points of conflict.

The question now arises concerning the theological consequences or consequences for theology that arise from this analysis of the discursive situation of theology as interdependent and oppositional. I want first to mention three available responses to the theological situation as I have described it that I believe are inadequate.

I

The first of these, under the slogan that "doctrines divide but service unites," elevates praxis over theology. While there will always be Christians for whom "hand" is more important than "head," that point of difference ought not to be distorted by a retreat from theology because of what I take to be the oppositional and even conflicted situation created by theological discourses. It impoverishes the tradition to develop a bias against one of the three "theatres" of Christian expression, to use Stephen Sykes's word. There will always be a theological component or aspect to Christianity, and it need not always be subordinated to action (or feeling). To do so will serve either to conceal it or to prevent its adequate development. Conversely, while social and political aspects or consequences are always actually or potentially present in theological discourses, I believe neither that those implications always outweigh or determine theology nor that failing to make social and political factors primary is itself an act that always should be interpreted as primarily political. Theologians, meanwhile, should recognize that Christians for whom the "theatre" of social and political analysis and action is more important than theological reflection will take an interest in theology that has been shaped by the goals of social and political analysis, critique and action, and such politically charted theologies will not fit well or fully into the discursive field as I have described it. Liberation theologians, for example, are likely to offend theologians of the sort I have used as examples in this study because theology that is determined by the need to analyze structures of oppression and to warrant action in response to them will strike theologians less politically engaged as unbalanced or partial, while they, in turn, will offend liberation theologians as insufficiently aware of injustice and of their own political attachments and implications. The three "theatres" are always in tension with one another, but they also are not separable. Theology is also a form of action; action carries feelings and theological convictions; feelings are confirmed by actions and clarified by theological reflection. I would call for no denigration of theology because of this study of its oppositional relations. Nor would I side with theologians who are offended by theologies directed toward the instigation or justification of social action or by those, for that matter, shaped by the third "theatre" of interest and determined by feelings of devotion or trust.

Hermeneutics offers a second answer to the problem created by the oppositional and conflictive situation created by theological discourses, but it is an answer that, as I argued in my previous book, is inadequate.[1] The hermeneutics of Hans-Georg Gadamer and Paul Ricoeur, for example, depend on an inclusive situation predicated on their own particular discourses. Moreover, such projects cannot avoid presaging ahead of language an actual, retreating horizon accommodating conflicting texts or worlds. Finally, they cannot adequately dissociate the narrative of an ever-expanding and inclusive world of meaning from the metanarrative of Western culture as legitimately and endlessly expansive and inclusive.

I am also unconvinced, thirdly, that the oppositional character of theological discourses can or should be resolved or transcended by an ecumenical theology. Theology cannot be elevated to some high ground above the dynamics of theological differences and oppositions. The reason is that there is no ecumenical theology able to resolve or transcend the differences that create the oppositions that I have described. A theology so crafted would have to be partial and selective. In addition, I think that these moves ahead or upward are in the wrong direction, for they mean an even greater degree of abstraction, a greater dissociation from and unawareness of the dynamics by which theological discourses are fashioned and refined. What this more inclusive theology would likely become is a kind of creedal fetishism or abstraction of symbols. It projects onto what is derivative the status of the fundamental and sustaining. Such a theology, while it will pretend to stand above the kinds of empowerment that should, I would say, be recognized—institutional and oppositional—will be engaged in one or the other mode of self-empowerment all the time. A theology that stands above the dynamics of differing discourses avoids the need of having or choosing a starting point, and it thereby deceives itself by the lure of an Archimedean privilege.

Not all projects in ecumenical theology are so easily given to abstraction as this brief sketch suggests, of course. An excellent exception, for example, is Oscar Cullman's *Unity Through Diversity.* What I like so much about this work is its recognition of the differences among churches, including differences that are irreconcilable, theological or theologically significant, and crucial to the identities of the particular churches. Cullman calls, in the face of the situation, for a "unity through diversity."[2] His stress is on the latter term, "diversity," because he sees the individuality of particular churches to be gifts of the spirit. St. Paul, using the metaphor of the human body, emphasized the importance of differing members of the body, even as he was arguing for the importance of the body's unity; Cullman shifts the metaphor to apply not to the individual persons that constitute a particular church but to the many churches together that constitute Christianity today.

Each church, then, in its particularity, is *the* church and has spiritual gifts, but the churches need one another for two reasons: first, they need to be reminded that other, differing churches also have spiritual gifts and that all of these diverse gifts come from the same spirit; and second, they need one another because particular churches, when left to themselves, can more easily distort and pervert their gifts. The presence of other churches not only reminds a church of other gifts but also reveals more easily than would otherwise be possible how and when the perversions of particularity creep in.

Cullman calls for a "federation" of churches, specifically for a council in which all churches would be participants without sacrificing their individuality. "I am thus in this manner," he says, "seeking to establish community by a process of mutual supplementation, perhaps even through obvious sharp contrasts" (73). In such a federation or council "*all churches, just as they are,* can find their place" (81).

I find this proposal an attractive one for three reasons. First, Cullman, while talking about institutions and practices, never loses sight of theological differences and conflicts that create and exacerbate the separations of churches from one another; second, he affirms the diversity, even the oppositional relations of churches and their theologies to one another; third, he does not ignore or dismiss the institutional complications of the ecumenical agenda. But his proposal fails to be theologically convincing, even though it can be recommended as a prudent course to pursue. It is unconvincing, among other reasons, because the unifying structure that he proposes, while it has, as he recognizes, no ecclesiastical identity or force, also has, as he does *not* recognize, no theological force or significance. As he says, "The community of churches for which this council is to provide the unifying structure would of course be a human institution, as I have already emphasized repeatedly" (60). This lack of theological significance and power not only makes the council he proposes theologically irrelevant; it also undermines Cullman's argument, for the Pauline metaphor that gives so much force to his argument for affirming diversity here works against him. Paul's stress is on the unity of the Church, and that unity holds a tremendous, even primary, theological force and significance for him. In contrast, Cullman proposes a solution to theological diversity and conflict that is theologically contentless.

II

More potential for response to the theological situation as I have described it may lie in so-called "narrative theology." But this option, while it holds much that is suggestive and salutary, usually subjects narrative to already established theological interests, rests on inadequate understandings of narrative, and fails to recognize that narrative also is discourse, that it is oppositionally determined.

I shall venture to say, first of all, that "narrative theology" seems often developed in response not to the largely narrative form of biblical texts but, instead, to the demands of certain theological interests. Theological interests appear to be protected, for example, by some narrative theology's interest in the "realistic" quality of biblical narratives.[3] The emphasis here is not so much on a particular style or mode of narration as on a certain way that biblical narratives can and should be read.[4] While the difference between "realistic" as descriptive of a kind of narrative style and "realistic" as a way of reading a narrative may be subtle, it has important theological potential because the latter, "realistic" reading, easily can warrant a certain kind of extratextual authority, namely the presumption of actuality. A realistic reading, rather than a taking into account the realistic effects achieved by a narrative, can become a reading that looks through a narrative toward that to which it refers, and, as Hans Frei and others have pointed out, this is the way in which biblical narratives have largely, although not exclusively, been read, both in conservative and liberal contexts. A narrative theology based on "realistic" readings of the narratives is a theology that subjects narrative to its own interest. Although the actual occurrence of things recounted in biblical narratives is or can be an important theological interest, theology is impoverished when another text, such as an historical reconstruction either of events and persons or of the faith or theologies of ancient Israel or the early Church, is substituted for the biblical narrative. The hermeneutical questions of whether or not to take what is depicted by a biblical narrative as having actually occurred or existed and of what criteria are employed to make that decision and to measure that consequence may be important for a narrative theology. What is at stake, here, is a theological reappraisal of reading. "Narrative theology" should address questions that concern reading biblical narratives; it becomes theologically less productive when it serves to warrant theological investments in certain kinds of reading.[5]

Another way in which "narrative theology" can be seen to protect particular theological interests is through the uses made of H. Richard Niebuhr's discussion of the attitude of the teller in the tale, the teller's relation to the material of the narrative.[6] This is an appropriate interest to take in narrative because a narrative always encloses a teller within it, and that teller always has a relation of some kind to his or her material—distant or near, approving or disapproving, impersonal or personal, etc. Niebuhr makes much of this aspect of narrative. He sets a sharp distinction between kinds of relations that tellers can have to their material. On the one side he places a personal relation to the material by which the teller treats characters in the narrative as subjects, by which the teller values quality, and by which time is duration and society is community, while on the other side he posits an impersonal relation to the material—characters are treated as objects, strength is valued, time is quantified, and society is determined by external relations. This distinction is based not so much on a theory of narrative, specifically on point of view, but on Martin Buber's distinction between "I–Thou" and "I–It" relations and on Josiah Royce's doctrine of loyalty and trust.

Before commenting on the theological interests determining "narrative theology" influenced by this distinction, I want to point out the rather minor role that this particular distinction plays in a more inclusive narrative theory. Indications of the presence of the teller constitute only one of four separable meaning effects of a narrative, and it is not always the most important. Furthermore, the signifiers in a narrative that indicate the teller can themselves be divided into three groups—choice of material, attitude toward or relation to that material, and language use or style. Niebuhr is principally interested in only one of these three effects, what I call attitude. Attitude, furthermore, has two aspects, a physical aspect, which is often called point of view, and an emotional/evaluative aspect. It is in the latter aspect of attitude that Niebuhr is principally interested. That is, his discussion of narrative is based on one of the two aspects of attitude, which is one of the three evidences of "tone," and "tone" is one of the four meaning effects or components of narrative discourse. While I do not discount the importance of this aspect in an overall theory of narrative, it is a rather small basis from which to speak of narrative as a whole and from which to make deep divisions between kinds of narratives. It should also be borne in mind that axiological questions such as raised by Niebuhr's treatment of narrative are not limited to narrative discourse but affect all discourses and human actions. Any text can be read as conveying or creating a relationship of loyalty and trust between the material and the speaker or reader. Even a list of rules or names can be recorded or read with a sense of deep personal involvement and celebration.

The theological interest that a narrative theology sponsored by Niebuhr's distinctions sustains is one that separates things Christian from their non-Christian context. The separation runs along the boundary that Niebuhr creates between the contrasting relations of the teller to the material, as described above. A sharp distinction and a nonrelation is sponsored, thereby, between matters internal to the Christian community, especially the stories that it values and reads in a certain way, and what lies outside it, including ways in which its story or stories are read by others.

I would say that Christian stories and Christian identity, like any other, are never only internal or isolated matters. Narratives of identity are dependent on external as well as on internal discourses. The stories that I or my group tell of other people who are unlike me or do not belong to my group fortify my or our identity as much as do stories that I tell about myself or about my group. Stories about other people, especially those for whom I or we have low regard, are indispensable to the process of self and group identity. Narratives secure value and identity both positively and negatively. This can be seen in biblical narratives, too. The narratives of Abel, Abraham, Isaac, and David (internal, mostly positive narratives with which the reader feels personally involved) depend upon and are bound to contrasting narratives of Cain, Lot, Ishmael, and Saul (external, more judgmental narratives in which the teller and the reader maintain or even increase a distance). It is, then, a mistake to discuss the formation of Christian identity, value, loyalty, and trust in and through narrative by focusing on only internal narratives. There are no Christians without negative narratives about others. Both inner and outer, internal and external, narratives go into the articulation of Christian identity. "Narrative theology" ought not to subject biblical narrative to an already established theological need to posit disconnections and nonrelations between Christians and non-Christians, Church and world, or Christian community and secular society.

A third theological interest that determines some narrative theology concerns history and time. A theological interest in history and time arises, of course, from other considerations as well—the Christian affirmation that God acts in history, that the history of the Church, its traditions and creeds, is authoritative, etc.—but the recent form this attention to narrative time takes often concerns ethical issues. At stake primarily—and Alasdair MacIntyre is the most substantial and influential voice in this discussion—is the wholeness of an ongoing life that tends to be lost in discussions of moral problems as atomistic and in analyses of decision-making applied to ethics.[7] A person's life has a wholeness, a unity, that relates past to future, and narrative can or does reveal that wholeness. Human actions, moments in life, intentions and desires should be seen in relation to this temporal or dramatic whole and, when treated in isolation or abstraction, should be recognized as having been lifted from a primary, complex, and continuing whole. The noticeable traces of Aristotle in emphases of this kind grant a complexity and an impressive ancestry. The implicit anthropology, the ethics, and the emphasis on narrative time are interdependent and mutually supportive. But the result, as with Aristotle and all who, in their narrative theory, follow him, from the Chicago neo-Aristotelians to Paul Ricoeur, will be an emphasis on narrative time or plot at the expense of the other interests, components, or languages of narrative discourse. True, MacIntyre and those influenced by him include considerations of character, setting, and even tone in their work, as does also Ricoeur, but the privileging of plot discounts the variability of narrative discourses, because any of these four languages, components, or meaning effects can be the most important in a particular narrative. Theologians who come to a discussion of narrative with an interest in temporality or human actions tend to isolate and emphasize aspects of narrative that support this theological interest. An overemphasis on plot and narrative time provides a third instance of narrative theology that subjects narrative to a theological interest.

The principal appeal of narrative theology is the wholeness or coherence that narrative can provide in contrast to the particular, various, and often conflicting propositions and assertions of theology. This appeal misleads when narrative becomes itself a kind of mental form, as it appears in Stephen Crites's often noted essay on the narrative quality of experience.[8] A kind of a priori status is given to narrative by Crites, and narrative is the way by which the experiences are ordered and retained by the mind. Narrative in such formulations becomes not a kind of discourse but the form of a mental work. However, when retained as a kind of discourse and not translated into a mental form, narrative can be recognized as capable of housing theological interests that, when abstracted from narrative, more easily become contraries and points of conflict. This commodious quality of narrative, the capacity, that is, of a narrative to contain differing voices and discourses without needing to have one dominate the others, has been described by no one so well as by Mikhail Bakhtin.[9]

III

The question of the relation of narrative to propositional theologies should now be raised, although it may not be easily answered. But two observations may be helpful. First, Roland Barthes argues that sentences resemble miniature narratives.[10] That is, noun and verb act like or stand in as character and action. I would say, instead, that sentences are potential narratives or distillations of narratives. I think that this situation is clearer when, instead of sentences and propositions, proverbs form the point of comparison. A well-known interrelation exists between proverbs and narratives, and anthropologists and folklorists are uncertain whether narratives in traditional societies are extended proverbs or proverbs distilled narratives.[11] In any event, the two, rather than exclude one another, seem to complement, require, and penetrate one another. Perhaps the same is true of narrative and proposition in theology. A propositional theology and a narrative theology may potentially depend upon one another. Not only are theological propositions found in narrative and narratives in propositional theologies; it can also be said that narratives are often expanded theological propositions and propositions condensed narratives.

While narrative theologies and propositional theologies require one another, a narrative theology cannot fully resolve or contain the conflicts that I have depicted as inevitable for propositional theology, because narratives, although commodious, are not so inclusive and complete as they are sometimes taken to be. This point anticipates what I shall be saying later about narrative as discourse. A story stands not by itself but as different from and in opposition to other stories. So, when one hears talk of *the* Christian story, as though that were something single, inclusive, and independent, one can only conclude that difference and divergence as characteristics of narrative discourses have been ignored or suppressed. As a matter of fact, Christianity is constituted not by one but by many groups each of which could have many stories told of it or could tell many stories about itself. And many of these groups have stories that they tell of one another. When the singular is used to refer to *the* Christian story, some kind of unity is being posited either above this diversity or somewhere within it. Christians do this because of the temptation of Platonism that is so strong for them. When Tatian, in his Diatessaron (150–60 C.E.), created a single narrative out of the four Gospels, and when that narrative became the authoritative text among Syrian Christians for centuries to come, this is a clear indication of the hold of Platonism on those Christians. The single narrative had the appeal of a higher form, a single story of which the four Gospels are manifestations or versions. When narrative theologians, then, refer to the Christian story or the story of the Christian community, one should think of Syrian Christianity from the second to the fifth century and its Platonist suppression of diversity and difference in favor of unity and wholeness.

Narrative theology, secondly, tends, as I have already implied, to work with an inadequate appreciation for the complexity and variability of narrative. I have tried to maintain in my work that narratives are constituted by multiple languages. These have to do with 1) the place, environment, and conditions of the narrative world (atmosphere), 2) people as individuals and in relationships (character), 3) actions and events in themselves and in their relations to one another (plot), and 4) the teller in the tale (tone). All signifiers in narrative discourse have meaning effects that can be related primarily to one of these four interests, components, or aspects of narrative discourse.

An important characteristic of these four sets of interests, or groups of signifiers, is that any one of them can dominate the others and deform them toward itself. While it is not unavoidable that this occur (a narrative may be constructed in such a way that all four have equal weight), it usually is the case that a narrative is dominated by one or two of these interests with the remaining sets of signifiers subordinated to the dominant. Narrative theology is distressed because, as has been seen, theologians enter the discussion of narrative already committed, by virtue of a philosophical or theological agenda, to one or another of these interests or languages of narrative and will subject the discussion of narrative to that preconceived and determining concern. Narrative theorists do the same.[12]

A further, major point about narrative to bear in mind is that each of the four areas of interests, or kinds of signifiers, constitutes a diverse and, I think, antinomic semantic situation. It is not possible fully to display the variables here, and I shall only suggest some of them. Beginning with the set of signifiers I have placed under the heading of "atmosphere," one easily discovers complexity and diversity. For example, place or environment can be personal, social, or physical, and narratives not only differ as to which of these is primary but also as to whether or not the boundaries of the human environment are narrow or extensive and whether or not the conditions of human life are favorable or unfavorable to the needs and desires of human beings. What can be said of atmosphere is also true of the other sets of signifiers in narrative discourse. "Plot": Is human time characterized primarily by its conformity to natural rhythms, to social and political interactions, or to personal, internal development? and are these processes creative and to be trusted, or destructive and to be resisted or fled? "Character": Are people basically nasty or good, reliable or unreliable, transformable or fixed, free or determined, individual or communal?[13] "Tone": What is worthy of attention, how should this or that material be evaluated, and to what degree does language create and reveal, or compromise and obscure understanding and relationships? All four distinguishable kinds of signifiers in narrative suggest matters that are uncertain not only because they are complex but also because they seem to be antinomic; contrary answers can be given to these questions. The conditions of our world are *both* destructive to and supportive of our needs and expectations; people are *both* mean and worthy; temporal processes are *both* destructive and creative, etc. A particular narrative, in order to be coherent, will pay attention to only some of the possible interests under each of the four headings and will tend to favor one answer to the several questions under each that I have raised. A particular narrative, therefore, will achieve coherence partly by eliminating or suppressing consideration of factors that could be used to support contrary answers or raise additional questions. In one narrative characters are reliable and transformable; in another they are nasty and fixed, for example. In one narrative the social environment supports human needs and desires, while in another people are coerced and reduced by social conditions. In one narrative events take a positive or upward turn, while in another they tend downward toward loss and destruction. In one narrative experiences are valued as rich in personal or social significance, while in another they reveal that human life is disappointing and vain.

The point particularly relevant to narrative theology concerns the diversity and conflict that result from these complexities. Narratives tend to be partial, to stress one set of interests at the expense of others, to provide one set of answers to an array of questions, and to disregard or suppress other interests, questions, and answers. This means that narratives are as much clarified in their meaning and force by the differences that exist among them as they are by their own internal coherence. Narratives are discourses, and they cannot be understood in isolation from one another. It is only by hearing other narratives that I begin to recognize what a particular narrative is. Narrative coherence depends as much on difference and exclusion as on completeness and inclusion.

I make these points about narrative, among other reasons, to encourage a certain reading of biblical narratives, because they are complex and diverse along the lines that I have drawn. That is, biblical narratives constitute a discursive situation marked by difference and even opposition. Biblical narratives differ from one another in terms of their dominant interests. For example, I have recently argued that plot dominates the Exodus narrative, that character is the dominant element in the narratives of Judges, that atmosphere dominates the Jonah narrative, and that tone is the dominant in the Gospel According to St. Mark.[14] So much is this the case that it can even be said that God appears in these narratives principally in and through their dominants. The dominants are, then, the differing centers of theological importance in these four biblical narratives.

Diversity among biblical narratives and texts is also revealed—and this is a matter more to the point of this discussion—by the differing answers given by them to those questions proffered above, questions arising from the four sets of narrative interests, or four kinds of narrative signifiers. So, in some biblical narratives, such as, say, the stories of the conquest in Joshua, the course of events is positive or creative; the land is purged and made habitable. But in other narratives, say, the story of Saul, the course of events is downward and destructive. In some narratives the social and political conditions of life are ultimately supportive, as in the Joseph narrative, while in others they are evil and untrustworthy, as in apocalyptic narratives such as Revelation. In some narratives characters are good and reliable, as in Ruth, while in others they are capable of great evil and folly, as in the stories of David's family. If one were to go through all biblical narratives and ask what is assumed or affirmed in or about all four of these areas of interests, a wide range of options would appear. Even within one kind of writing, the wisdom, for example, there are sharply differing assumptions and affirmations: Is the world we live in basically predictable and supportive of our attempts to live wisely and righteously in it, as in Proverbs, or are these conditions unpredictable and apparently unrelated to our efforts to live wisely and righteously, as in Job?

Furthermore, the appearance of God in narrative form is related to the uncertainties and antinomies suggested by each of the four sets of narrative interests or signifiers. God appears in all four of the languages of biblical narratives because all four of these languages indicate areas of both great interest and great uncertainty. The matters suggested by them need to be addressed, but they are too complex and antinomic to be resolved and settled once and for all by the language of a single narrative. These four areas, sets of interests, or signifiers, are all crucial to the articulation of a narrative world or of personal or group coherence, but they are all problematic and questionable. This combination of the unavoidable and the uncertain creates a potent situation, a threshold, I would say. The appearance of God in narrative form occurs at these thresholds, and narrative discourse is as much a defense against as a conveyer of mystery. Biblical narratives, then, hide as much as they reveal God.

A narrative theology can counter the tendency of propositional theology to construct understandings abstracted from these complications, conflicts, and uncertainties. A narrative theology can resist the attempt to bring independently and abstractly constructed ideas to a reading of biblical narratives. It calls, instead, for reading narratives in such a way as to recognize the mysteries with which they deal, the thresholds between the familiar and the uncertain, to which narratives lead us and from which they shield us. A narrative theology should be a reading of biblical narratives, to the extent that this is possible, without some distinct idea, for example, as to what God is like, so that coherent propositions about God can be challenged by the combined uncertainty concerning God's ways and force produced by the sundry narratives. A narrative theology, rather than enlist in a campaign to protect theological interests, to ensure Christian coherence, or to produce certainty, will serve instead to challenge and subvert Christian certainty, coherence, and identity. A narrative theology will take narrative discourses as liminal places where, like Jacob with the night visitor at the Jabbok brook, one wrestles in order to obtain not only a name (an identity, coherence, or a theology) but also, if not more so, an injured hip, a chronic instability.

IV

From this perspective biblical narratives as well as theological discourses are diverse and conflictive, involved in an interdependent dynamics of opposition both among themselves and between one another. It is hoped that this analysis, combined with my previous book, will offer a way by which both biblical narratives and Christian theologies can be read, the relations among their internal interests traced, and their points of opposition with differing discourses, propositional and narrative, clarified. It is also hoped that this analysis reveals that a biblical narrative, a theological discourse, or a Christian's story cannot be taken as autonomous and that the diversity and opposition of discourses, upon which a particular discourse depends, must be taken into account. A discourse derives power and significance from its positive and negative relations to others, both to those it largely resembles and confirms and to those it repudiates, represses, or ignores. When conflicts between differing theologies, biblical texts, and Christian stories arise, theologians and other Christians should not view these conflicts with impatience and frustration or as unfortunate, unproductive glitches. Rather, the inevitability and productivity of such conflicts can now be recognizable, and the traditions behind differing discourses can be traced.

In addition to this set of general consequences that follow from this study, there are a few more directives or consequences for theology that should be mentioned. They are consequences that follow from the assumptions and proposals that earlier I clarified as basic to this study, consequences I shall adumbrate under the rubric "the language or culture of scripture and belief."

Theologians, by sharing the assumptions and propositions basic to this study, enter what I take to be an important cultural situation. As determining for theology in the modern period as the culture of reality and certainty was, so determining for it will be the recognition in our own time of the nature of discourses. This recognition questions authorities that in Modernism became deeply entrenched and stoutly defended, such traditional authorities as science, history, or reason. It now becomes clear that such authorities cannot be validated and stabilized simply by appeals to the realities to which they refer and upon which they depend or to the scholarly attitudes and interests that voice them but are principally established and authenticated by the discourses that advance their interests. It becomes clear, furthermore, that all discourses carry beliefs as to what should be included in an adequate account of the world, what is true, and what constitutes acceptable behavior. It may not be too much to say that discourse analysis and the assumptions upon which it is based lead not only into the politics of oppositional relations but also into the culture of belief. This opens up a large discursive situation that theological discourses can enter without a sense of intrusion. Theological discourses need no longer depend upon other discourses—historical, scientific, or philosophical—as though those others were in positions to provide a certainty upon which theology needed to depend or to which theology had to defer if it were to be taken seriously by thoughtful people.

The culture of belief emerges when attention shifts from the references of discourses, their voices and sponsors, and stabilizing structures beneath or below them to discourses themselves as forces in historical situations related to one another by interactive, social dynamics. The stability, continuity, and degrees of agreement required for such a situation to be viable are provided not by something external or antecedent to the situation but by the discourses themselves. For discourses have embodied within them a multitude of assumptions and beliefs—not all of which are in or can be brought to a participant's awareness—concerning what is good or evil, important and not important, real or fanciful, durable and dispensable, about values, authorities, goals, and the like.

This culture of belief is fully and consistently described and argued by Stanley Fish, especially in his recent collection of essays entitled *Doing What Comes Naturally.* Fish balances his "reader response theory," that is, his insistence that interpretations of texts are constructed and argued by readers rather than found in or derived from texts, with an equally strong insistence that reading is determined by sets of directives, assumptions, and beliefs that characterize "interpretive communities," communities that are often and most characteristically identified by him as professions, especially the literary and legal professions. These communities or professions are defined by Fish primarily by their practices, and the practices of these communities of interpretation set limits to and give tacit directions for interpretive acts. Those limits are not only the explicit methods of such communities and what those who practice them would say if asked what they do and why they do it in the way they do but also the innumerable beliefs and assumptions that practices imply and upon which they depend. Fish argues against the notion that these beliefs are derived from something external and antecedent and against the notion that they can be made conscious and examined, for even if they were made conscious and explicit they would be replaced by other tacit assumptions and beliefs that would allow for and support the action of examining and criticizing beliefs and assumptions.

While I agree with Fish's description of the role of belief in discursive situations, I disagree with him at several points. The most obvious, given the preceding study, is on the kind of stability or unity that he seems to impute to interpretive communities. As I said earlier, communities as institutions have embodied in them differing and often conflicting discourses. For example, there seem to be discourses that need always to be hidden or denied, that are contrary to acknowledged discourses by being less ideal or more self-serving, for example, and that create duplicity in, it seems, all institutions. Furthermore, discourses seem more to need one another and to constitute a discursive situation the more they differ from and conflict with one another. It is repudiation and repression that mark a discursive situation, and Fish's use of "interpretive community" and "professional practice" conceals both the duplicity created by the embodied discourses of an institution or practice and the conflict upon which discourses depend for their power and significance. I also disagree with the sharp division Fish makes between texts and interpretive communities, the one so indeterminate and the other so determining. Fish, as I said, needs to stress stability or unity in interpretive communities because it balances the indeterminacy of texts. But texts are not so discontinuous with their interpreters. The range from stable to unstable, determinant to indeterminant, duplicitous to straightforward, marks the "texts" of the interpreters' assumptions and beliefs as well as the texts that are being interpreted. I shall return to this point.

On the other hand, the situation Fish describes and that I am calling the culture of belief, one in which theological discourses now can and should find or locate themselves, I fully affirm. It is a situation in which all knowledge is dependent upon and attached to belief. There is no knowledge based on brute fact or derived from pure reason. Knowledge is always implicated with power and belief. And theology is no exception.

The price for admission to this situation is a sacrifice of special claims. A theological discourse cannot attack other kinds of discourses for denying their dependence on belief by imputing authority to fact and reason and then try to establish itself by appeals to the stability of "The Christian Community" or the "Christ event." If "history" or "fact," "reason" or "universal rules of logic," invoked as authorities for other discourses, are to be revealed by the theologian as products and projections of the discourses themselves and not separable from or antecedent to them, the theologian cannot, then, turn around and appeal to the objects of theological discourses or their sponsoring sources as granting a grounding, however spiritual, that warrants the discourses. To put it another way: Because the sources of authority in other discourses are vulnerable to critique does not mean that theology, because its referents and voices, its sources of authority, are different from those of other discourses, is exempt from the same treatment. An analysis that questions the status of "fact" or "reason" as independent of discourses does the same for "God" and "faith."

I am not suggesting that the general discursive situation into which theological discourses, having paid this price, now enter is an enclosed verbal universe, a walled coliseum of battling discourses severed and isolated from all that is "real" or "extant." While it is the case that the "real" is never available to us apart from language and is conditioned, even constituted, by language, this does not mean that language, as one of my colleagues put it, "is all there is." What needs to be questioned is the assumption that discourses establish a relationship between preexistent things, in the case of theology, between faith and the object of faith. The sources and objects of faith are extrapolations from Christian discourses rather than already established points between which theology forms a bridge. But to say this is not to deny the reality or importance of faith's sources and objects. It is, rather, that theological discourses carry belief within them, are statements of faith, and it is redundant to characterize them as such. Whatever we feel called upon to include in an adequate account of ourselves and our world, whatever arises in our discourses, is real and important for us. It is redundant to say that theology, by including the word "God," asserts that an adequate account of or response to what is real or important must include "God," and it is redundant to say that such discourses assume and assert the reality, power, and importance of "God." Our discourses take precedence over any prediscursive situation that might be imagined, such as subjects establishing what should be included in an adequate account of the world or what does and does not have power or importance. Questions such as "Do you think that what you speak of exists or is important?" interrogate the beliefs carried by our discourses and cannot be answered by appeal to some situation construed as free from interpretation. An uninterpreted world is unavailable to us. But this does not mean that interpretations create a world and cause things to exist. To put the matter in Derridean or perhaps anti-Derridean form, one could say that there is always presence or present time, although one cannot refer to presence or present time without textualizing it into absence or into past or future; we have no access to present time or presence without the textuality of past and future or of absence. As St. Augustine suggested, time does not become a problem until we begin to think about it. So, too, I go around making observations about my world and meaning what I say until someone (or I) asks, "Does all that you include in your account of the world exist?" or "Do you really mean what you just said?" Then I pause and wonder about such things. I emerge on the other side of the interrogation including this and that in my account of the world and continuing to believe that what I say is true.[15] The cultural situation in which theological discourses now move, then, is marked not by the articulation and defense of certainty or even coherence but by the articulation and defense of beliefs.

This does not mean theologians can expect that what they believe or the basic beliefs carried by their discourses will be shared by that culture. Theologians can ask, "Do I really believe that what I speak of exists?" or "Do I really believe what I am saying?" and they may find themselves answering, "No." *A fortiori,* a theologian may encounter interlocutors in the culture of belief who do not believe the things stated and implied by his or her discourse. That all believe means neither that all believe the same thing nor that all beliefs will be taken seriously. An important theological task, then, is to determine what beliefs we share in the culture of belief, what beliefs are unnecessary or not really believed, and what beliefs are worth contending for, knowing all the time that such interrogation itself depends on beliefs and can never be complete.

The culture of certainty and coherence was a culture of identity. The culture of belief does not make the marks of identity and coherence central. Indeed, Christian identity—and I take the phrase to be partly oxymoronic—may require a sense of autonomy and certainty that is an illusion and that actually depends upon difference, exclusion, and repression. The need to define and defend identity is an important effect of the preceding culture. It becomes less important when attention shifts to discourses. Identity, we now can see, is imposition, a social demand characteristic of a complex and officially (but not actually) egalitarian society. In such a society social categories and distinctions tend to be absolutized. The pressure to declare a Christian identity, therefore, is not Christian pressure. Much of what we feel in this regard is the need to categorize and be categorized in order to control and be controlled. Much of the compulsion for Christian identity and coherence comes not from the call to witness and be faithful but from the social demand that we check one of the boxes on application and other forms next to "Religion," that we distinguish ourselves as individuals or a group, that we use Christianity to serve a need for a social identity and a sense of distinctiveness, and that we become subjects to ourselves so that others can be objects. It may also be possible to interpret the call for Christian distinctiveness as masking a desire to stand out from or above a world that is becoming more crowded, more complex, and, in many ways, more difficult to understand.

What becomes clear, after release from the addiction of identity, is that things are authoritative, real, and valuable for people because they believe them to be so. What nonfoundationalism and postmodernism adumbrate is a culture characterized not by appeals to certainty, fact, the indisputable, and the actual unconditioned by belief but, rather, a culture characterized by shared and differing beliefs.

The culture of belief is steadied by textuality and it should be called the culture of scripture as well as of belief. Since I argued in my previous book for the location of every person or group somewhere on the textual field and proposed the term "scripture" to designate that location as an alternative to the contraries of "canon" and "writing," I shall not repeat that argument. I will simply assert that every person, group, and society has scriptures, that is, texts that grant and articulate their world's contours, contents, possibilities, and norms.[16] I shall now return to the point that I made in passing when I described Stanley Fish's contribution to delineating the outline of a culture of belief. I would say that those beliefs are latent, potential, or incipient texts and that the texts that we read and interpret are related in manifold negative and positive ways to those texts or scriptures. A text that I can read and interpret is never only and wholly out in front of me; it is related somehow to my scriptures, and I would almost say that a text is always to some degree something I already know, something I am already in, and never wholly indeterminate.

In my previous book I addressed the more specific question of Christian Scripture and the many factors that assure the complexity and uncertainty of Scripture as a basis for Christian identity and coherence. I discussed primarily the variability of biblical narrative discourses and the way in which they take away as much as grant coherence and identity. I also mentioned the wide cultural diversity and tensions in the Bible, the great temporal stretch and cultural inclusiveness of the Old Testament, and the terribly complex cultural situation of the New, particularly the crisscrossing of Jewish, Greek, and Roman factors with Christian in the New Testament. Finally, while dealing almost exclusively with biblical narratives, I also mentioned the generic diversity of biblical texts and the differences and uncertainties that diversity of genre creates.[17]

To all of this now can be added the differing theologies that I have described in this study. For these differences, as I already have said, arise not only from the components of theological discourses and the capacities each carries to become a dominant but also from the biblical texts themselves. Although I have typified their positions in order to make the points of emphasis and differences clearer, it becomes possible to say not only that prophet, priest, and sage lived in related, but clearly distinguishable, theological worlds but also that the texts that can be designated in these three ways are not only distinguishable from but potentially or actually in conflict with one another.

What I want to do is to affirm these qualities of Scripture and theology. In other words I take the complexity, diversity, and oppositions of the biblical texts to be of great theological importance and the conflicts among theological discourses to be of great biblical importance. For by taking seriously these characteristics, it becomes recognizable that biblical and theological discourses have coherence and unity by being partial and that the larger Scriptural and theological situation carries within itself the seeds for its own deconstruction. For incompleteness and uncertainty are as important for belief and discourse as are their contraries.

The implications, finally, for thinking of the relations of Scripture to institution should also be clear, whether that institution is a church or a denomination or of a less specific kind, such as "The Christian Community." Attempts to subject or house Scripture within an institution are attempts to impose a coherence and identity on texts that are set up as much to deny as to support such coherence and identity. For an institution, as I said earlier in this study, is an embodied or tacit discourse. What David Kelsey has said of doctrines of Scripture, that they are determined by individual theologies more than by Scripture, can be said of any attempt to house or subject Scripture to church, denomination, or Christian community.[18] Scripture gives rise to churches and the discourses inscribed in them. Churches are housed by Scripture, not Scripture by churches.

I do not mean by this that one ought to abandon theology and church affiliation in acknowledgement of the diversity and conflicts of scriptural and theological discourses. No, there is a need for coherence, affiliation, and identity, too. But, bear in mind, they are always partial, temporary, and dependent.

NOTES

Preface

1. "Although theory emanated largely from other disciplines, it was in a profound sense *literary* theory: Foucault, Derrida, Lacan, and Lyotard all made frequent and self-conscious use of the putatively undisciplined and nondiscursive imagination of literary texts in their alliance against the certainties of their own discourses and disciplines" (Bruce Robbins, "Oppositional Professionals," in Jonathan Arac and Barbara Johnson, eds., *Consequences of Theory* [Baltimore: Johns Hopkins University Press, 1991], 2).

2. Reinhold Niebuhr, *Human Destiny,* vol. 2 of *The Nature and Destiny of Man: A Christian Interpretation* (New York: Charles Scribner's Sons, 1949), 148–56.

Introduction

1. Jeffrey Stout, *Ethics After Babel: The Languages of Morals and Their Discontents* (Boston: Beacon Press, 1988), 240.

2. For a discussion of "basic beliefs," see Terrence W. Tilley, "Response Epistemology and Religious Foundationalism: How Basic Are Our Basic Beliefs?" *Modern Theology* 6, no. 3 (April 1990): 237–58.

3. Michel Foucault, *The Archaeology of Knowledge,* trans. A. M. Sheridan Smith (New York: Random House, 1972), 34.

4. I am indebted to Professor Tilley for raising the question of the relation of these differing discourses to one another in a letter to me.

Chapter 1

1. See, for example, Teun A. van Dijk, ed., *Handbook of Discourse Analysis,* 4 vols. (Orlando: Academic Press, 1985).

2. Donald E. Allen and Rebecca F. Guy, *Conversation Analysis: A Sociology of Talk* (The Hague: Mouton, 1974), 27.

3. See Harvey Sacks, "Notes on Methodology," in J. Maxwell Atkinson and John Heritage, *Structures of Social Action: Studies in Conversation Analysis* (Cambridge: Cambridge University Press, 1984), 26.

4. Michael Riffaterre, "Compulsory Reader Response: The Intertextual Drive," in Michael Worton and Judith Still, eds., *Intertextuality: Theories and Practices* (Manchester: Manchester University Press, 1990), 56–78, 77.

5. Diane Macdonell, *Theories of Discourse: An Introduction* (Oxford: Basil Blackwell, 1986), 33.

6. Jean-François Lyotard, *The Postmodern Condition: A Report on Knowledge,* trans. Geoff Bennington and Brian Massumi (Minneapolis: University of Minnesota Press, 1979), 10. Lyotard goes on, in a footnote, to say, "I place them [speech acts] within the domain of the *agon* (the joust) rather than that of communication" (88).

7. Michel Foucault, *Power / Knowledge: Selected Interviews and Other Writings 1972–1977,* trans. Colin Gordon et al. (New York: Pantheon Books, 1980), 142 and 151–52.

8. Michel Foucault, *Discipline and Punish: The Birth of the Prison,* trans. Alan Sheridan (New York: Random House, 1979), 136–38.

9. Lyotard, *The Postmodern Condition,* 17.

10. Fredric Jameson, *The Political Unconscious: Narrative as a Socially Symbolic Act* (Ithaca: Cornell University Press, 1985).

11. Nancy Fraser, *Unruly Practices: Power, Discourse, and Gender in Contemporary Social Theory* (Minneapolis: University of Minnesota Press, 1989), 64.

12. Michel Foucault, "The Discourse on Language," trans. Rupert Swyer, in *The Archaeology of Knowledge* (New York: Random House, 1972), 216.

13. Jameson limits "institution" to the "externality" of a group. See *Postmodernism, or The Cultural Logic of Late Capitalism* (Durham: Duke University Press, 1991), 322–47.

14. *Theories of Discourse,* 12.

15. Fraser, *Unruly Practices,* 63.

16. For an excellent study of the situational, institutional, and political characteristics of all sciences and knowledge, see Joseph Rouse, *Knowledge and Power: Toward a Political Philosophy of Science* (Ithaca: Cornell University Press, 1987).

17. See Stanley Fish, *Doing What Comes Naturally: Change, Rhetoric, and the Practice of Theory in Literary and Legal Studies* (Durham: Duke University Press, 1989), esp. "Profession Despise Thyself: Fear and Self-Loathing in Literary Studies," 197–215.

18. Ibid., 163–79.

19. William A. Christian, *Doctrines of Religious Communities: A Philosophical Study* (New Haven: Yale University Press, 1987), 14.

20. Reinhold Niebuhr, *Moral Man and Immoral Society: A Study in Ethics and Politics* (New York: Charles Scribner's Sons, 1960), 51–82.

Chapter 2

1. Richard Rorty, *Philosophy and the Mirror of Nature* (Princeton: Princeton University Press, 1979), 10.

2. Richard J. Bernstein, *Beyond Objectivism and Relativism: Science, Hermeneutics, and Praxis* (Philadelphia: University of Pennsylvania Press, 1983), 203. The previous section will have made clear, I hope, why I am uneasy with the terms "community" and "conversation" as used by Rorty and Bernstein.

3. See Stanley Fish, *Is There a Text in This Class? The Authority of Interpretive Communities* (Cambridge: Harvard University Press, 1980), 241–43.

4. For an excellent analysis of and response to this split in the work of Rorty, a split between what he construes as a Romantic as over against a Pragmatic impulse, see Nancy Fraser, "Solidarity or Singularity? Richard Rorty between Romanticism and Technocracy," in Jonathan Arac and Barbara Johnson, eds., *Consequences of Theory* (Baltimore: Johns Hopkins University Press, 1991), 39–63.

5. Kenneth J. Gergen, "Warranting Voice and the Elaboration of the Self," in John Shotter and Kenneth J. Gergen, eds., *Texts of Identity* (London: Sage Publications, 1989), 70–81. See also Michel Foucault, "What Is an Author?" in Paul Rabinow, ed., *The Foucault Reader* (Middlesex, England: Penguin Books, 1986), 101–21.

6. John Carlos Rowe, "Structure," in Frank Lentricchia and Thomas McLaughlin, eds., *Critical Terms for Literary Study* (Chicago: University of Chicago Press, 1990), 23–39.

7. Diane Macdonell, *Theories of Discourse: An Introduction* (Oxford: Basil Blackwell, 1986), 9.

8. George A. Lindbeck, *The Nature of Doctrine: Religion and Theology in a Postliberal Age* (Philadelphia: Westminster Press, 1984), 68–69.

9. See A. J. Greimas, *Structural Semantics: An Attempt at a Method,* trans. Daniele McDowell et al., Introduction by Ronald Schleifer (Lincoln: University of Nebraska Press, 1983).

10. Mark C. Taylor, *Erring: A Postmodern A/theology* (Chicago: University of Chicago Press, 1984).

11. See, e.g., H. Richard Niebuhr, *The Social Sources of Denominationalism* (New York: Henry Holt and Company, 1929).

12. Pierre Bourdieu, *Distinction: A Social Critique of the Judgement of Taste,* trans. Richard Nice (Cambridge: Harvard University Press, 1984).

13. Stephen Sykes, *The Identity of Christianity: Theologians and the Essence of Christianity from Schleiermacher to Barth* (Philadelphia: Fortress Press, 1984).

14. Fish, *Is There a Text in This Class?,* 13.

15. Frank Kermode, *The Genesis of Secrecy: On the Interpretation of Narrative* (Cambridge: Harvard University Press, 1979).

16. Sykes, *The Identity of Christianity,* 27.

17. Nicholas Lash, *Theology on the Way to Emmaeus* (London: SCM Press, 1986), 115, 116.

18. Frederick Herzog, *God-Walk: Liberation Shaping Dogmatics* (Maryknoll, N.Y.: Orbis Books, 1988), xii.

Chapter 3

1. For a discussion of the nature and role of "hidden" premises in argumentation, particularly as to how they differ from "missing" premises and "unstated" or "unrecognized" assumptions, see Trudy Govier, *Problems in Argument Analysis and Evaluation* (Dordrecht, Holland, and Providence, R.I.: Foris Publications, 1987), 98–99.

2. See Roman Jacobson, "The Dominant," in Ladislav Matejka and Krystyna Pomorska, eds., *Readings in Russian Poetics: Formalist and Structuralist Views* (Cambridge: MIT Press, 1971), 82–87.

Chapter 4

1. Karl Barth, *Learning Jesus Christ through the Heidelberg Catechism* (Grand Rapids, Mich: William B. Eerdmans Publishing Company, 1964), 33, 67, and 138.

2. Karl Barth, *The Doctrine of God,* vol. 2 of *Church Dogmatics,* trans. G. W. Bromiley et al. (Edinburgh: T. and T. Clark, 1957), part 2, 163; and Karl Barth, *The Humanity of God,* trans. John Thomas and Thomas Wieser (Richmond, Va.: John Knox Press, 1963), 38–46.

3. *The Humanity of God,* 48–49.

4. "The Gift of Freedom," in *The Humanity of God,* 69–75.

5. *Dogmatics in Outline,* trans. G. T. Thomson (New York: Philosophical Library, 1949), 116.

6. "Evangelical Theology in the Nineteenth Century," in *The Humanity of God,* 11–14.

7. Karl Barth, *Protestant Thought: From Rousseau to Ritschl,* trans. H. H. Hartwell (New York: Simon and Schuster, 1969), 306–54.

8. Ibid., 355–61.

9. Karl Barth, *The Doctrine of Reconciliation,* vol. 4 of *Church Dogmatics,* part 1, 576.

10. Karl Barth, "The Time of Revelation," chap. 14, part 2, vol. 1, of *Church Dogmatics,* 45–122.

11. *The Doctrine of God,* vol. 2 of *Church Dogmatics,* part 2, 346.

12. Søren Kierkegaard, *Attack upon Christendom,* trans. Walter Lowrie (Boston: Beacon Press, 1956).

13. Karl Barth, *The Doctrine of the Word of God,* vol. 1 of *Church Dogmatics,* part 2, 48.

14. *The Doctrine of God,* vol. 2 of *Church Dogmatics,* part 2, 345.

15. *The Doctrine of Reconciliation,* vol. 4 of *Church Dogmatics,* part 1, 516–17.

16. Jürgen Moltmann, *Theology of Hope: On the Ground and the Implications of a Christian Eschatology,* trans. James W. Leitch (New York: Harper and Row, 1967), 16.

Chapter 5

1. D. M. Baillie, *God Was in Christ* (New York: Charles Scribner's Sons, 1988), 36–38.

2. Leonardo Boff, *Jesus Christ Liberator,* trans. Patrick Hughes (Maryknoll, N.Y.: Orbis Books, 1979), 264–78.

3. Hans Küng, *The Church* (Garden City, N.Y.: Doubleday and Company, 1976), 21–24.

4. Cardinal Joseph Ratzinger, " 'Consecrate Them in the Truth': A Homily for St. Thomas' Day," *New Blackfriars,* no. 803 (March 1987): 112–15.

5. "The Cardinal, in Summary," an interview by Vittorio Massori of Cardinal Joseph Ratzinger, *New Blackfriars,* no. 780 (June 1985), 262–70, 264.

Chapter 6

1. William James, *The Varieties of Religious Experience: A Study in Human Nature* (New York: Collin Books, 1961), 397–99.

2. William James, "The Will to Believe," in *The Will to Believe and Other Essays in Popular Philosophy* (New York: Longmans, Green and Co., 1897).

3. William James, *A Pluralistic Universe* (London: Longmans, Green and Co., 1916), 328–30.

4. Henry Nelson Wieman, "Transcendence and 'Cosmic Consciousness,' " in Herbert W. Richardson and Donald R. Cutler, eds., *Transcendence* (Boston: Beacon Press, 1969), 153–63.

5. Henry Nelson Wieman, *The Source of Human Good* (Carbondale: Southern Illinois University Press, 1946), 56.

6. Bernard Eugene Meland, *Faith and Culture* (Carbondale: Southern Illinois University Press, 1953), 40–43.

7. Bernard Eugene Meland, *Realities of Faith: The Revolution in Cultural Forms* (New York: Oxford University Press, 1962), 187.

8. *Faith and Culture,* 125.

9. *Realities of Faith,* 196.

10. Walter Rauschenbusch, *A Theology for the Social Gospel* (New York: Macmillan, 1917), 178.

11. Reinhold Niebuhr, *Moral Man and Immoral Society: A Study in Ethics and Politics* (New York: Charles Scribner's Sons, 1932).

12. Reinhold Niebuhr, *The Nature and Destiny of Man: A Christian Interpretation,* vol. 1 (New York: Charles Scribner's Sons, 1949), 53.

13. Ibid., vol. 2, 299.

14. *Moral Man and Immoral Society,* 97.

15. Langdon Gilkey, *Naming the Whirlwind: The Renewal of God-Language* (Indianapolis: Bobbs-Merrill, 1969).

16. Josiah Royce, *The Problem of Christianity* (Chicago: Henry Regnery Company, 1986), vol. 1, 1–47.

17. Ibid., vol. 2, 208–14.

18. Ibid., 272–73.

19. Ibid., vol. 1, 178–79.

20. Ibid., vol. 2, 428–29.

21. Ibid., 423–24.

22. H. Richard Niebuhr, *Radical Monotheism and Western Culture* (New York: Harper and Row, 1960), 11.

23. Shubert Ogden, *Christ Without Myth: A Study Based on the Theology of Rudolf Bultmann* (New York: Harper and Row, 1961), 137.

24. Shubert Ogden, *The Reality of God and Other Essays* (New York: Harper and Row, 1970), 31.

Conclusion

1. For a more complete statement of my reservations concerning these hermeneutical projects, see my discussion of Gadamer and Ricoeur in *Story, Text, and Scripture: Literary Interests in Biblical Narrative,* 72–84 and 100–102.

2. Oscar Cullman, *Unity Through Diversity,* trans. M. Eugene Boring (Philadelphia: Fortress Press, 1988).

3. See Hans W. Frei, *The Eclipse of Biblical Narrative: A Study in Eighteenth- and Nineteenth-Century Hermeneutics* (New Haven: Yale University Press, 1974). I cite this influential book because of the attention it draws to the realistic style of biblical narratives and not because it protects theological interests.

4. Cf. Hans W. Frei, "The 'Literal Reading' of Biblical Narrative in the Christian Tradition: Does It Stretch or Will It Break?" in Frank McConnell, ed., *The Bible and the Narrative Tradition* (New York: Oxford University Press, 1986), 36–77.

5. See my *Story, Text, and Scripture: Literary Interests in Biblical Narrative.*

6. H. Richard Niebuhr, "The Story of Our Life," in *The Meaning of Revelation* (New York: Macmillan, 1962), 43–90.

7. See Alasdair MacIntyre, *After Virtue: A Study in Moral Theory* (Notre Dame: University of Notre Dame Press, 1984).

8. Stephen Crites, "The Narrative Quality of Experience," *Journal of the American Academy of Religion* 39, no. 3 (September 1971): 291–311.

9. For a discussion of the narrative theory of Bahktin see my *Modern Fiction and Human Time: A Study in Narrative and Belief* (Tampa: University of South Florida Press, 1985), 183–88.

10. Roland Barthes, "An Introduction to the Structural Analysis of Literature," trans. Lionel Duisit, in *New Literary History* 6, no. 2 (Winter 1975), 241.

11. See, e.g., C. L. Sibusiso Nyembezi, *Zulu Proverbs* (Johannesburg: Witwatersrand University Press, 1963), 4–5; Dwight Edwards Marvin, *Curiosities in Proverbs* (New York: G. P. Putnam's Sons, 1916), 67–87; Archer Taylor, *The Proverb and an Index to the Proverb* (Copenhagen: Rosenkilde and Bagger, 1962), 27–31; and Paul Hernadi, *Beyond Genre: New Directions in Literary Classification* (Ithaca: Cornell University Press, 1972), 156ff.

12. For an extended discussion and illustration of this situation in narrative theory see my *Story, Text, and Scripture,* 50–97.

13. My use of such terms as "character" in reference to various meaning effects of narrative is not vulnerable to the critique lodged by Fredric Jameson when he says, for example, that Lacan's work poses problems "for any narrative analysis which still works with naive, common-sense categories of character, 'protaganist,' or 'hero' . . . " because I use such terms only as ways of referring to kinds of narrative meaning effects rather than to convey certain ideologically weighted notions of the individual and his or her ontological or social standing. See Fredric Jameson, *The Political Unconscious: Narrative as a Socially Symbolic Act* (Ithaca: Cornell University Press, 1981), 153.

14. *Story, Text, and Scripture,* 24–49.

15. This formulation of the matter was stimulated by a comment that Joseph Rouse makes in *Knowledge and Power:* "To say that the things we deal with in our everyday actions exist is redundant in much the same way that saying the sentences I assert are true is redundant" (156). I would amend the statement to read, "The statement that I believe in the existence of that which I include in my account of the world and that I believe what I say is true is redundant."

16. See *Story, Text, and Scripture,* especially 131–33.

17. Paul Ricoeur makes much of the interactions among differing genres in the Bible. See, e.g., *Paul Ricoeur: Essays on Biblical Interpretation,* ed. Lewis S. Mudge (Philadelphia: Fortress Press, 1980).

18. See David H. Kelsey, *The Uses of Scripture in Recent Theology* (Philadelphia: Fortress Press, 1975), 150.

INDEX